IT'S YOUR MOVE

Daring to be really intimate with friends, lovers and family can be as frightening as it is rewarding unless you understand and face your own fear for what it is. *GETTING CLOSE* gives you the tools for understanding, and the techniques for going beyond fear to a whole new way of relating to others.

Richly and perceptively illustrated with actual case histories, this is the new book that *leads you through the changes*. All you do is take the risks. And reap the rewards!

GETTING CLOSE

BARBARA FAST

Barbara Fast

Getting Close

Daring To Be
Really Intimate
With Friends and Lovers

A BERKLEY BOOK
published by
BERKLEY PUBLISHING CORPORATION

This Berkley book contains the complete
text of the original hardcover edition.
It has been completely reset in a type face
designed for easy reading, and was printed
from new film.

GETTING CLOSE

A Berkley Book / published by arrangement with
G. P. Putnam's Sons

PRINTING HISTORY
G. P. Putnam's Sons edition published December 1978
Berkley edition / December 1979

ISBN: 0-425-04265-0

A BERKLEY BOOK® TM 757,375
Berkley Books are published by Berkley Publishing Corporation,
200 Madison Avenue, New York, New York, 10016.
PRINTED IN THE UNITED STATES OF AMERICA

For Julie:
husband, lover, friend and intimate.

Acknowledgments

Melissa, Daniel, Jennifer, Timothy, Bob, Julius, Betsy, Drs. Ruth and Robert Shapiro, and all those others who answered questions and gave intimately of their feelings, experiences and themselves.

Contents

Introduction

We all want intimacy. We long for it and talk about it constantly. And yet we throw up all kinds of barriers to it when it comes along. We are afraid of it, we distrust it even while we search for it.

Our desperate need to share is made all the more acute because of the feelings of loneliness and isolation that we all experience at least at one time or another. However, in this fast-moving, technological society in which the nuclear family has replaced the extended family, many people cannot find the strength to reach out to touch and love another person.

Over and over again I hear the desperate cries, "I wish I could be close to someone!" "If only I could have a sexual relationship with someone I could love and trust." "If only I could have warm, loving friends or an understanding, deeply committed union with my husband [or wife]." "I need to know I'm not alone!"

Just what is this closeness that we so strongly desire and yet resist?

Intimacy isn't limited to sex and marriage. It must be an integral part of any human life style, and a part of each and every relationship we engage in. It's a learned behavior that starts the moment a child is born and continues throughout his life, but it is also something any individual can develop and enhance at any stage in his life. It is the ability to reveal innermost feelings, thoughts, and emotions to someone else without becoming anxious or afraid. It is the ability to *enjoy* being open as well as the ability to enjoy the openness of someone else without judging that person.

Intimacy is a very special bond which exists between two people, a bond which nourishes us as individuals, yet allows us to share joys and accomplishments as well as pains and sorrows. It makes both members of an intimate relationship more than each one can be individually, and yet it strengthens the two in their own identity when they are apart.

Unfortunately, facing the challenge of intimacy is tremendously difficult for most of us. We feel that involving ourselves with another leaves us exposed and vulnerable. We say to ourselves, "If I enter an intimate relationship and it ends, I'm bound to suffer. Why should I take the risk?" There is the fundamental paradox to intimacy.

We want it. We can't live without it, but we seem to be afraid to risk it. But we *can* learn to take the risk. We *can* learn how to communicate with others on a deep, richly rewarding, emotional level.

We also can learn to be intimate with ourselves, not only to find that our inner fears and vulnerabilities are unfounded, but also to discover a new source of strength, comfort, and creativity within each of us.

We can learn that part of living is taking risks. To avoid risks is to avoid life. And to avoid intimacy is to live a little less.

One

What Intimacy Is

Intimacy is a mutual sharing of inner feelings and private emotions. It requires not only trust but also acceptance, respect, caring, and understanding. When you are truly intimate with another person, you can reveal yourself without fear of reprisal. Two intimate people may not always agree, but they must understand each other.

How do we know when we have problems with intimacy? How do we know when we are afraid to risk it? The fear of intimacy betrays itself by its own unique symptoms. The following questions are warning signs. Do any of these ten danger signals relate to you?

1. Are you an insulated person, uptight, controlled in your body movements?

2. Are you constantly angry with the person or persons closest to you?

3. Do you use sarcasm, teasing, or put-downs?

4. Is your life a timetable, so filled with routine that you feel panic at the thought of doing something different, going someplace new, meeting new people?

5. Do you arrange your life so that you are always busy, involved with organizations or outside activities? Are you seldom alone with yourself or with your family?

6. Do you find it hard to feel or show emotion?

7. Are other people often angry at you?

8. Do you need approval constantly?

9. In social situations, must you have a few drinks before you feel comfortable?

10. Do you have a vague feeling of anxiety most of the time?

If you have any of these symptoms, you most probably suffer from a fear of being intimate.

The Loneliness of Twosomeness

Sometimes we can live in what the world assumes is intimacy, and yet we can be completely isolated. In a bitter divorce case, a judge asked a wife, "You've been married eighteen years, Mrs. Elroy. How many children do you have?"

Moving uncomfortably in her chair, Mrs. Elroy said, "I have three."

"What are their ages?"

"Fourteen, ten, and eight."

The judge nodded. "In the last eight years, have you had intimate relations with your husband?"

This was a delicate but highly significant moment in the proceedings. Mrs. Elroy looked up, her lips tight. "Do you mean sexual relations, Judge?"

Impatiently the judge answered, "Sexual, intimate—whatever you care to call them."

There was a long pause, and then the woman shook her head, her eyes suddenly filling with tears. "We've had sexual relations often, but we have never been intimate."

For the judge it was a sad revelation, one of those sudden moments of insight which makes us all stop and reflect. Later, discussing the case with a colleague, the judge asked, "What is intimacy? How can you define it? Is intimacy different things to different people? You share a house, a bed, children, a life with another person as that woman in court did. And yet she shared all of these things with her husband for nearly twenty years. She shared sex too. Yet now she realizes that she was never intimate with him. Something was desperately lacking in their relationship."

In another court case a husband told his lawyer, "There's no way I can make it with another person. And if I do get into another marriage it's going to start all over again. We'll play the *I-put-you-down, You-put-me-down* game, and it will be another hate relationship instead of a loving one. So much for intimacy!" His marriage had lasted for two years.

Sad as these couples are, there are others who won't take the risk at all, reasoning that if you don't make the commitment you won't be hurt. An airline stewardess explained, "I'm not going the marriage route. I have affairs. The last one was long and passionate. I saw Alex three or four times a month. As long as he was in Houston and I was in New York it worked. No one got hurt. Maybe I just can't live with anyone and be that close—even though I want to very much!" She shook her head sadly. "I wonder if I will ever get it together with anyone? I never even felt close to my mother or father!"

The airline stewardess took what she felt was the safest route—no risk at all. Had she taken a chance, even a small one, she might also have taken the first step to a caring relationship.

* * *

False Sounds and Phony Touches

These people I just mentioned are not unusual. They're like many of us in today's world: we have no idea of what true intimacy is. We never saw it between our parents, nor were we ourselves treated intimately by our families—yet we know what we want but do not have in intimacy.

One problem people frequently have in forming intimate bonds is that too often they use words and gestures to reach a state they confuse with intimacy. Certain words suggest a sense of closeness, and these words are then substituted for intimacy itself. Listen to the people around you, hear what happens when you cut through the charades and empty talk and *really* listen.

"Darling! I've missed you terribly."—He met her once at a cocktail party.

"Man, we just got to get together soon."—They had a business deal a month ago.

The greetings are effusive with intimacy words, but neither has any intention of going further than words.

"I feel uncomfortable kissing all the women at every social get-together," a very sophisticated middle-aged man named Mathew said. "It's meaningless. It's gotten so that it isn't even a sign of friendship. With my friends, you come into a party, and it's *sweetheart* this and *darling* that and *kiss, kiss, kiss!* Half the time you don't even connect. And now with the men there's a new thing. They hug! It just makes me uncomfortable."

We have all been programmed to give simulated or false gestures of intimacy: the mutual hugging, the unrelated kisses, the hand-holding, even the handshake which has been translated into mere ritual. We shake with our right hand and grasp a shoulder or arm with our left, give a "sincere" stare and send the message, "*I feel close to you!*"

What the act really says is: *I may not know you, but it doesn't matter so long as this simulated gesture fools you—and fools me too.*

Even if you expect a lack of intimacy from such casual acquaintances, what about the mother who tells her child, "Mommy is always your best friend"? These are intimate words, but the child understands that what her mother really means to add is, ". . . as long as you do what I tell you to, and behave the way I want you to."

What about the father who says to his son, "You can come to me and tell me anything." His hand is on his son's shoulder, but his eye has wandered to the TV set in the corner. ". . . Tell me only what I want to hear" is left unsaid, but the son knows his father is preserving an illusion of intimacy without becoming involved. How? By using the right words.

Is this illusion of intimacy, this false intimacy, so bad? Doesn't it at least comfort us and let us cope with the problems of life? Sometimes, perhaps, but false intimacy is a trap. Ultimately, it leads to isolation and alienation.

More and more men and women confess to a sense of emptiness and a longing for a close relationship with another person or other people. No matter what the age group or the background the cry is the same: "I need an intimate relationship." "I want to feel close to someone." "I wish I had a friend, a real friend." "If there was someone I could trust, someone who would trust me . . ."

I want, I need, I wish. There is an overwhelming inability in so many people to enjoy a husband, a wife, a lover. People are unable to get close to friends or to their own families. They feel adrift, isolated, unfulfilled. To be unattached, to belong to no one, is equated with being unloved.

In desperation, the unattached search for someone, anyone, to make their lives meaningful. In big cities the search will often take young men and women to the singles bars. These young people may remember a college fraternity, a high school club—remember what they thought was a warm and friendly group with intimations of intimacy. Now, out in the "real world," they try to recapture or simulate that feeling. In the crowded bars they forget that the closeness is only physical and masks an inability to break through emotional shells.

In the bars the words suggesting intimacy flow like honey. *Darling. Sweetheart. Beautiful, baby, beautiful, I dig you.* The gestures too seem too intimate—a quick feel, a furtive grope, a violation of privacy with hands and arms—as if these outward symbols could force emotional closeness.

But the intimacy turns out to be *only* physical. The people around the bar, the probing eyes and hungry mouths, are all so desperate, so in need of intimacy, that men and women must get together in bed that very night just to prove that they are really sharing an intimate experience.

"Listen, I can score with four different chicks a week!" The young man's tone is boastful, but behind the boast there is a terrible desperation. "I walk away and I don't even know the chick's name. Most of the time it isn't even worth the effort."

A young woman, fresh from a divorce, says frantically, "I know he'll call. I mean, we really had something going!"

What she and her new conquest had going was sexual contact without emotional closeness, and it only served to make the disappointment more bitter and the longing more desperate. They have learned the gestures and the language of pseudointimacy, and they are clinging to the illusion that it is the real thing. They talk frantically and they go through the mechanics of sex, hoping that the others will fill the emptiness within themselves and eradicate the loneliness. And yet each word, each gesture, is driving a wedge of alienation that forces the couple farther apart. Each one is afraid to open him- or herself up to another, afraid to trust and be trusted.

Mutual trust is one of the basic tenets of intimacy. But all too frequently our early experiences in the family do not prepare us to trust others nor to confide in them. Cindy grew up in just such a household without the ability to trust. During her childhood her father had been laid off at the plant where he worked. Cindy was told nothing about it, nor about the family's money problems.

"Children shouldn't worry about those things," her father insisted. "It's really not her business."

Sensing that something was wrong, seeing the worried looks and whispers passing between her parents, Cindy felt isolated. She was worried about her parents and their unspoken tragedy, yet she wasn't allowed to express her worried, unhappy feelings. Instead she reacted with a violent attack of allergy.

Cindy could not disclose a private, sensitive part of herself—her fears and anxieties. Such a disclosure is an important part of intimacy. In a family, as in a later relationship between lovers, self-disclosure must be accompanied by the knowledge that sharing one's innermost thoughts and feelings will not put one in danger. Everyone must feel safe within the relationship, safe to the degree that he or she will not be put down or hurt by what has been said.

Cindy's parents could not share the unhappy parts of their life with her, and they gave her the impression that such sharing was wrong. Years later, when Cindy became pregnant by a boy in town, she was unable to entrust this experience to her parents to share that trouble with them, to turn to them for the help she desperately needed.

When you are truly intimate with someone else,

there is the ability to share the good and the bad with no sense of engulfment or entrapment. But sharing is not taking over and losing your identity.

Intimacy Is Not Fusion

Another danger in a family situation—or between lovers—is the very opposite of Cindy's problem. There can be too much closeness, too much dependence. Parents or lovers can overwhelm and suffocate a child or partner. This becomes fusion.

In essence, fusion is complete oneness with another person. It is also the absolute inability of either person in a relationship to operate in an independent fashion. We've all heard friends talk about fused people in admiring terms. "I swear, those two never disagree." "My mother and I go everywhere together. She's my best friend . . ." or "They're such nice people. They really don't need anyone else but themselves. They like to listen to each other, and they couldn't care less about the rest of the world . . ."

But all such relationships wear thin very easily. Those who are that close come to know everything about the other person. There is nothing new and exciting to discover. They can't be surprised or delighted—or even disappointed with them. Their alter ego becomes boring and rapidly loses charm. The people involved are too close—in fact, they are so close they are fused.

In a fused relationship, if one of the partners starts to move toward independence—a grown child who decides to get a place of his own, a wife who goes to work, a husband who wants a night out with the boys—the other partner feels threatened and immediately demands oneness again. Fusion does not allow either individual to grow or change. The relationship feeds on itself, destroying both of those involved. Fusion is a form of false intimacy.

Intimacy Is a Delicate Thing

Just as fusion may lead to false intimacy, so sharing space and time may become true intimacy. Two people who have been intimate for many years very often take on each other's characteristics—yet retain their own sense of self and privacy. I can think of a happy, older couple who lived next door. The wife seemed to have the same smile as her husband. She would use her hands the way he did, and the older the couple grew, the more they seemed to take on each other's ways. In a very subtle fashion, a truly intimate couple will often imitate the gestures and words of one another.

We must remember that intimacy is not just sharing the good things; it involves the bad feelings as well, the entire spectrum and exchange of feelings. It involves anger, irritability, illness, the aches and pains of growing old, and all the stresses of daily life. If you can share *all* aspects of life, then you are well on your way to discovering true intimacy.

Fully realized, mature intimacy also consists of sharing the intensely happy emotions as well: a beautiful sunset, a child's first steps, a sexual encounter—just as much as the sad moments of grief and loss. In times like these, intimate people are together in the same space and time, and because they respond to life in the safe company of each other, they become able to experience truly close, meaningful moments.

When I first started to do researching for this book, I asked my daughter and her husband what they thought true intimacy was. After some joking, my son-in-law, Dan, finally said, "I'm not quite sure. I only know that I feel most intimate with Jennie when she cries. It doesn't happen very often, but when it does I see her as she is, with all her defenses stripped away. I feel I know her then."

As he said it, he reached across the table and took Jennie's hand. It was a small, revealing gesture, and in a way it was the beginning of a deeper intimacy between them.

Jennie said, "What he is saying is that when I drop my guard and open up, when I become vulnerable to him with my tears, I am trusting him."

Dan nodded. "It's true. I wanted her to trust me. I sometimes feel she holds back too much."

"Now we're working on it." Jennie smiled. "Someday I'll be able to show myself without tears."

What We Want from Intimacy

In my search to discover the meaning of intimacy I questioned friends and strangers about what they wanted from an intimate relationship. I spoke to students at college, to working men and women, housewives, and professionals.

Among the women, the quality mentioned most often as important in intimacy was *sharing.* Among the men it was *the ability to open up to another.* The other qualities mentioned most often by women were *the ability to communicate without fear of rejection* and *nonphysical closeness*.

The other qualities of lesser importance mentioned by women were *openness, trust, independence, caring, commitment, listening, confiding, respect, understanding, nonanxiety, interest in me,* and *physical closeness.*

The women, unlike the men, were well aware of

the dangers of fusion, of losing themselves in their lovers. They asked for independence along with commitment. They asked for respect and understanding, qualities men seemed to take for granted. As if they were commenting on the battle between the sexes, many frequently asked men for the ability to listen.

Curiously, none of the women mentioned love. Do women take love for granted? I feel that women associate love so closely with intimacy that they do not bother to list it as a separate attribute.

Among the men, after the ability to open up, the following qualities were cited in this order: *trust, honesty, accepting another's thoughts and feelings without judgment, protection, nonphysical closeness, love, caring,* and *sex.*

The qualities these men sought seem to knock all our truisms off their feet. The rash of men's magazines, the macho principle, advertising and literature all tell us that sex is man's prime concern. Those answering my questions put sex last on the list. Do most men take it for granted, or do they, as I believe, really want something deeper and more meaningful than a sexual relationship?

None of the men listed *confiding, listening, independence, commitment, respect, understanding, nonanxiety, interest in me,* or *physical closeness.*

Women, on the other hand, wish to approach intimacy on a positive level. They are more willing than men to be open. They want to *share,* to *trust,* to be *independent,* to be *listened to,* to be *able to confide,* to be *understood.* They have a *sense of commitment*, and they want to be *respected.*

Women were willing to be the initiators in a close relationship, and perhaps they were more liable to take the risks in an intimate situation.

The men I questioned were concerned with *self-protection*, being *accepted,* and not being *badly judged.* They wished to be *responded to.* They saw themselves as the *recipients* of intimacy, not the *initiators*.

What I found most intriguing was that so many people I questioned, men and women, told me they could not talk to each other, they could not communicate on a "meaningful level."

"No matter what I say, he hears something else."

"She doesn't understand what I mean."

"It's the *way* he says it."

Behind the complaints, the frustration, the bewilderment, I sensed a desire to be heard and understood. I became aware of how important communication is in reaching any degree of closeness or intimacy. So many things we mean to say are left unsaid—so many things we do say are misinterpreted.

Two

Why We Fear Intimacy

Three Who Were Afraid

Most people who are afraid to get involved with another put up emotional, psychological, and even physical barriers to cover up deeper, underlying problems, problems that often go back to their early childhood. We will offer excuses, often very acceptable ones, as a superficial way of dealing with a deep hurt. But excuses keep us from looking too deeply into our own motivation, from recalling the pain and vulnerability of childhood.

In questioning many people who had fears about intimacy, I was struck by some common refrains:

"I'm afraid of being rejected."

"If I trust her, she'll betray me."

"I just can't make it with a guy. I'm too dumb . . . too scared . . . too ugly . . ."

"If I really let her get close to me, she'll find out what a bastard I am."

In almost every case, fears such as these come from childhood hangups, from family situations where relatives we were close to rejected us, hurt us, or betrayed us. When it happened again and again, we began to create devices to avoid intimate situations where rejection, hurt, or betrayal might ever conceivably occur.

Children are vulnerable and ill equipped to assert themselves. Their self-esteem can be easily damaged, and they can go through life using old neuroses to frighten intimacy away. The following are three cases where just such fears caused people to build barriers that were designed to protect them against other people:

In her late twenties, Kathleen was a slim, dark-haired woman with a gentle, waiflike quality. "The one thing I really want," she insisted, "is a close relationship with someone I can talk to, confide in, and trust. But it never works out that way. I guess it's because I'm so tired and exhausted all the time. I come home from work and I just want to crawl into bed."

As she talked, Kathleen referred to her weariness again and again. Everything about her suggested it. The way she walked, stood, and sat all said that life was too much for her. "I'm depressed because I'm exhausted all the time." After a moment, she added, "I feel so depleted."

Kathleen was a researcher for a small insurance company. When she first came to work, she was asked to join some of the women for bridge, but she was too tired to accept the invitation after the day's work. One woman suggested dinner and a movie, but Kathleen refused, telling her she wasn't up to it. A few eligible men in the office dated her once or twice, but seldom called back. Eventually the invitations stopped. Her listlessness was an effective barrier to any kind of friendship.

What Kathleen didn't understand was her own terror of intimacy. She herself closed off all the avenues to a close relationship, or even the possibility of a simple friendship.

If it hadn't been for a doctor, a consultant for her company, she might have gone on blaming her inability to make close friends on her weariness, depression, and physical exhaustion. At the doctor's insistence she had a complete physical checkup. The results were all negative, and he suggested group therapy.

At first Kathleen resisted, insisting that she just needed some more vitamins or a little extra iron, but finally she agreed to give the group session a try. "The first few meetings were terrible," she said. "I don't know where I got the energy to make it out to the group after work. It took months before I could turn the *tired, tired, tired* messages off in my head."

A year later Kathleen developed enough insight to begin to deal with her problems and to understand just how she used exhaustion as a barrier to closeness. "All my life," she told me, "I've been afraid of being hurt. I expected everyone to lie to me, to act the way my parents did. I expected them to say one thing while they did something else. I had to start trusting people. I had to learn that if I'm disappointed or hurt once in a while—that's not the end of the world. I can't retreat into exhaustion or sleep the way I used to when I was a child. I have to cope with people and my own feelings."

Jerry was another person afraid of intimacy, but his fear took another form. The image he presented to the world was that of the frenzied, eager but successful beaver. Still in his forties, he had held five different jobs in the past ten years. Jerry moved with incredible speed, not only physically, but in and out of jobs as well. He walked fast, ate fast, and drank. And, as his wife complained to her close friend, "My God, he's even too damned fast in bed!" Jerry was frightened of being still. At a party he would embrace everyone, moving in on friends and strangers, engulfing both with gestures and words. In a social situation, Jerry and his wife would arrive together, but as soon as they entered the room they were separate. She moved as far away from him as possible, and he, fortified with a drink, would zero in on anyone who would stand still for his jokes and chatter.

Jerry was so afraid of intimacy that he protected himself behind a barrier of endless words. This verbal assault effectively isolated him and prevented him from exposing himself to any real human contact. Even though his method was different, Jerry used words just as Kathleen used depletion and fatigue to avoid intimacy.

As a third case, consider Betty. Betty was a very giving, generous person. She could be very funny, but most of her humor was directed at herself. In spite of her extroverted personality, Betty had a deep fear of intimacy, a fear that caused her to wall herself in with a fortress of fat.

"I have no will power," Betty would protest. "I go on a diet and I stay on it for two months, and then I don't know what happens. I just can't stick it out and I start eating again like there was no tomorrow."

Betty had been taking weight off and putting it back on for most of her life. Two years ago, in a relatively thin period, she got married. Within six months she gained fifty pounds!

She berated herself for her lack of will power and her laziness, but the more she talked about losing weight, the fatter she got. "I feel like a balloon," she would say to her husband. "It's as if someone keeps pumping me up!"

Like many men and women who use fat as a fortress, Betty began to run scared once she took off enough weight to make her look attractive. Her vulnerability buzzer went off, and she started overeating again.

Here we have three people who feared intimacy and used three different devices to guarantee that they wouldn't become intimate. Why were they driven to these extremes? Why did they fear something so desirable? Each one would tell you, if you questioned them, that they really wanted intimacy.

The devices Kathleen, Jerry, and Betty used were extreme. Kathleen saw that she used exhaustion and a lack of energy to avoid intimacy, but what she couldn't understand was why she feared it. To find out she had to take a closer look at her background.

As a child, her parents told her, *Trust us. We love you.* But when she did trust them, she always found out that her trust was misplaced. Eventually, and rightly, she stopped believing them. This became a continuing pattern throughout her childhood. *Trust me!* her parents would say. But when she did, she was bitterly disappointed. Eventually she got the real message—*Don't you dare trust us.* She stopped trusting them, and unfortunately stopped trusting everyone else as well. Kathleen eventually discovered that when she was very tired, her parents left her alone. She began to associate tiredness with privacy. She withdrew into her physical exhaustion. What better device could she have invented to insure that no one would want to be intimate with her.

Jerry, the frenzied, constant talker, on the other hand, feared intimacy because he felt that if people really got to know him they would *find him out.* What was there to find? His carefully guarded secret became almost pathetically apparent once Jerry was aware of it.

When Jerry was six years old, his mother caught him in sexual play with his sister. A rigid, angry woman, his mother became furious and held the incident over him as a threat. "Wait until I tell your father. He'll punish you. God will punish you too. You're a filthy, bad boy and everyone will find you out!"

She never did tell Jerry's father, but she used the incident to blackmail him over and over again. In turn, Jerry withdrew from any close contact with his mother. Throughout his life he kept withdrawing and moving fast, talking incessantly. He never gave anyone a chance to be intimate enough with him to *find him out*. "I really am a bastard," he kept telling himself. "If my boss or wife or friends ever knew what I was like . . ."

What he was really saying was, "If my father ever knew!"

Jerry's unconscious fear of being *found out* had crippled him and made him unable to get close to anyone. Eventually his defense, his fevered activity, became more than his wife could stand. They separated, and afterward Jerry realized that the separation confirmed what he had always known and felt deep inside—he was no good, worthless. Now his wife had found him out, but he hadn't really deserved her in the first place.

Jerry is unable to go too deeply into the reasons why he feels the way he does. It's too painful and frightening, so he continues living at a frantic pace, hiding behind a barrage of words and acts, effectively punishing the little boy of his childhood by denying the man a chance for loving intimacy.

As for Betty, her fortress of fat was her last defense. Within it she hid her vulnerability. She truly thought that she wasn't worthy of love or affection. She didn't deserve it. If people really knew her they couldn't love her.

What made Betty the way she was? In truth, Betty was afraid of her own sexuality. As a child, her overly loving father kept comparing her to her mother, in a sense making her compete with her mother. As an adult, she equated being attractive, that is, being intimate with anyone, with being intimate with her father—and as a consequence—with betraying her mother. The answer? Never let anyone know her, hide the real Betty from the world behind all that fat.

When Betty lost some weight and began to receive a few compliments, panic set in. She went back to the ice cream sundaes and the raids on the refrigerator. The fortress would go up again and she would be safe!

Betty will always have a weight problem unless she learns to understand the underlying reasons that cause her to overeat.

She has tried all the crash diets, but none worked for long. She's been a dropout from dozens of weight control groups, and it was only recently, when one of the leaders of such a group asked her, "Why are you scared of being pretty?" that Betty began to realize that it was more than a lack of will power that was keeping her fat.

She tried to shrug off the question, but she couldn't deal with the sudden panic she felt when the woman from the diet group confronted her. Later that day she thought about it and again the anxiety and panic returned. Her first impulse was to go to the refrigerator and open the door. Standing there, she suddenly remembered her father and she burst into tears.

That night her tears became hysteria, and her bewildered and frightened husband insisted that she see a doctor. It took a while before Betty could even talk about her feelings toward her father when she was a child. The fear, anxiety, and guilt that welled up in her were all too painful.

Eventually, when she learns to understand why she

uses fat to avoid intimacy, she may be able to accept her own sexuality—not as a dangerous threat, but as a normal part of herself, and she will be on her way to being a woman instead of a defenseless little girl.

This, of course, is only one example of why people use fat as a defense against intimacy, even as there are other reasons for using frenzy or exhaustion besides the ones Jerry and Kathleen use. The strange and sad thing about all these devices is that they are often reflections of childhood hurts and fears, and while we may forget or bury many of our painful memories, it is not so easy to bury the feelings and emotions associated with them.

Among the people I have talked to about intimacy, I found that there were many who were able to make the connection between the way they acted today and the way they had acted as children and thus overcome their problems. One woman said, "I just can't trust older women. I always feel uncomfortable and insecure around them. I think it started with my grandmother. She brought me up, you know, but she was a terror. I watched her devour my mother and wreck their marriage. Now, anytime I begin to be friendly with an older woman I remember my grandmother. My tendency is to freeze up and move away. I have to make myself remember that all women are not my grandmother, and some actually wish to see my life go well."

A young man told me about his father. "I was never able to be close to him. I think it was because he was so domineering. I was afraid he'd take over and make all my decisions for me. Now I have to watch myself."

"What do you mean?" I asked.

"I'm just afraid of people taking over. I have to watch myself on the job. I have trouble taking supervision and being part of a team. It's that old fear of my father."

Both of these people understand the way their childhood relationships influenced their adult lives. Most of us don't have this insight. We react blindly to certain situations and often hurt ourselves. But all of us have the ability to explore our own feelings to try to discover whether they originate in the present, or as a reflection of the past.

The Contracts We Make

Frequently our fears of intimacy cause us to wall ourselves off from others, as Kathleen, Jerry, and Betty did. Often these fears drive us to make agreements or contracts with an intimate other. These contracts can be one of two kinds. One is destructive, negative, and unconscious. It is the hidden contract we make out of fear. It is bad because part of the contract is to keep the lid on our true emotions. Because of this, hidden contracts often breed resentment, anger, and even hate.

The other kind of contract is conscious and positive, an *upfront* contract. It is usually good because it is out in the open and available for negotiation. Either party is free to express his or her feelings about it.

Most of us are aware of the contracts our friends make. We have all seen parents who don't want to know what their children are doing. They're afraid such knowledge will force them to take action and become involved. Husbands and wives may make a contract not to discuss their teenage son's extra money. How and where did he get it? If they confront him, they may find his answer devastating, and they'd have to do something about his drug dealing. Better a silent contract to ignore it, they feel.

Then there are the lovers who have a hidden contract to ignore those nights when she says she must have dinner with her mother. They both know the affair is in trouble.

Or there's the marriage where sex has fallen apart but a hidden contract says, neither of us must mention it.

To understand just how such a contract works, let's take a look at a married couple, Frank and Helen, upwardly mobile and in their midthirties. Helen is a small, dynamic woman, full of life and energy. Frank, a heavy-set, deliberate man, is very much the master in his own home—but always awkward in social situations.

Before an executive's cocktail party for his company, Frank would tell Helen, "Don't worry. I can handle these guys."

Frank sounded assured, but Helen knew from experience that he was easily frustrated by large gatherings. His track record for remembering names was terrible. Helen, who never forgot a name, would nod cheerfully, but she knew that at the party his "handling of the guys" would depend on her.

Smiling brightly, she greeted the boss before Frank could, and she'd make sure that he heard her greeting. "Of course I remember your wife, Mr. Block. Just the other day Frank was telling me what a wonderful job Mary is doing in the PTA," she would say.

Helen kept at it, throwing Frank all the cues, but always making it look as if he were in control. Inevitably, she couldn't help but resent her unappreciated role, but to ask for appreciation would unmask the entire charade.

Frank and Helen thus had a hidden contract, but neither of them acknowledged it. Keeping it hidden allowed resentment to build up—on Helen's part because she gets no credit, and on Frank's, because he knows he can't make it alone. Eventually this hidden contract becomes a block to intimacy.

A *positive* contract between the two would work this way. Frank would say, "Look, Helen, I'm a bitch at remembering names. I always forget the name of my boss's wife—maybe because it's his third. I just panic when I meet so many people. Damn it, I hate these big affairs!"

"I'll stick close and clue you in, honey," Helen might say.

"What would I do without you?" Frank would answer. "Thanks."

This would be a conscious, upfront contract. Both Helen and Frank would know what was expected of each other, and what they owed to one another. They would be honest about the help they gave and got. This is a positive agreement in a caring, non-threatening relationship.

Another example of a hidden contract is one where a husband earns less money than his wife. Here, the unspoken agreement is that she can earn more provided that he dictates the way it is spent. After all, he is the *Lord and Master* in the house. But the contract is never discussed because it would be too threatening to both. Their lack of intimacy leads to a restricted amount of honesty. They're both locked into sex roles. He's the *Boss* and she's the *Little Woman.*

With many hidden contracts, there is an even further danger: the threat of blackmail. One case involved a daughter in her late teens who discovered that her mother was having an affair. She knew why, but she never openly confronted her mother with what she knew. In her family she had learned, at an early age, that you got things by manipulating others. She had watched her mother do it to her father, and she too had learned the game. In a subtle way she let her mother know that she was onto her.

"Did you enjoy the bridge game Wednesday?" she would ask. Behind the seemingly innocent question was the unspoken threat. *I know what you were doing, where you went, and I won't let Dad know. In return you mustn't give me a hard time about where I go and what I do.*

The mother in this case agreed to this unspoken blackmail, and thus entered into a hidden contract. But both mother and daughter paid a price. All bonds of true closeness were severed. They never discussed anything personal. It became an estranged, hands-off relationship. They were both afraid to let it be anything else because intimacy would have forced both of them to face up to what the other was doing.

Eventually a contract like this one destroys real love and intimacy.

Life Changes

So far we have seen some conscious and unconscious ways in which we set up barriers to intimacy. Sometimes, the barriers occur because of a change in life situation. Many couples find, for instance, that when their children grow up and leave home, the marriage begins to fall apart. The complaints come from both sides.

"He's been retired for six months and I can't stand him underfoot all the time," she says. "At least at work I had the guys to talk to and kid with," he retaliates. "I never knew how little we had in common. We were never alone that much. At least with the kids home there was something to talk about at meals."

These complaints came from couples who have stayed with a marriage only because of their family. They have erected a pretense of intimacy and even believed it themselves. When their situation changed, they were unable to change with it. Now, suddenly, there seemed to be nothing to hold them together. Divorce, or staying together in an unhappy marriage appeared the only two alternatives. They really had no intimate relationship at all.

The reverse of this relationship is one in which a couple had true intimacy during their marriage and now when the children are grown and on their own, and the financial responsibility is lightened, they find that the shift in life style can actually bring more freedom and intimacy. As one couple in this type of marriage confided, "We rediscovered sex in the afternoon! It's the way it was when we were first married, before the kids came."

The couple had always had a good sex life, and they've been close, and truly intimate all along. But all the normal pressures of raising a family and managing a home had pushed sex into a minor role. With most of the pressure off, they could rediscover their old roles. Instead of being Mommy and Daddy, they could become lovers again.

This is a positive approach to life. This husband and wife aren't concerned with aging. The wife isn't too fearful of losing her looks because she's secure in her relationship. She knows her husband loves her for more than her appearance. In turn, the husband has no need to find renewed youth in the eyes of a younger woman. Each has always related to the other honestly, and they have experienced intimacy without hangups or fears. They share their life knowing that they can trust and rely on each other, yet neither loses touch with his own unique self.

Sometimes life shifts and changes are due to health

problems. One woman, after a mastectomy, suddenly found that she was terrified of having sex again with her husband. "How can I let Dick see me like this? He was always so proud of my figure! I was never ashamed to undress in front of him, but now . . ." Her voice trailed off. "Part of me is gone. I'm not a whole person."

Some men and women are victims of a society that is so body-conscious that it equates a woman herself with her breasts. A woman who absorbs this message loses a part of her identity when she loses a breast. She becomes less of a person, she thinks, and so is not worthy of intimacy.

For men, one of the most difficult changes to weather in terms of intimacy is a heart attack. What used to be an old man's disease is attacking younger and younger men in our pressurized society.

After a heart attack, both partners face a difficult adjustment in resuming sex. Whether a doctor advises sex or forbids it, it still poses a potential threat and a fear in both partners' minds. "If I really let myself go, won't it be a strain on my heart?"

The fear is bound to limit intimacy, even when a man receives a medical all clear.

Like physical changes, there are other life situations that can affect intimacy. The lovers living together who thought they were close may find that marriage, with its commitments and responsibilities, tears apart what they thought would last forever. The birth of a first child can create the beginning of an intimate family and strengthen the bonds between a husband and wife—but it can also weaken those bonds. The changes caused by parenthood, the additional worries and expenses, can be too much to handle. Sometimes the simple fact of a third person, the new baby, may force a different life style that neither is able to adjust to.

A new job or a move to a different neighborhood, an injury or illness, losing one's job, a new responsibility at work, even something as minor as a missed vacation can create enough problems to damage intimacy.

Not all changes bring a lessening of intimacy. Some men and women are able to handle change in their life situation and come out of it more intimate than before. It helps if both partners are understanding and caring, and if the relationship has always been close. Single people manage, too, if their own self-worth is high enough.

Mr. Cool Meets the Little Woman

James Bond, a prototype of an ultimate style in masculinity, is so debonair and worldly wise that he feels nothing. He makes love to a beautiful woman and three pages later she is brutally murdered. How does Bond react? He shrugs and goes on to the next encounter.

As the story progresses, he is tortured, disfigured, and shot at and his women are taken from him, but inevitably he goes through it all without losing his composure.

How do we read the author's message? It's simple. Be cool. Don't ever show your feelings. Jump in and out of bed, but never allow your emotions to get in your way. And, above all, don't get involved with anyone emotionally.

Bond is presented to us as a super hero, a man we can all model ourselves on—if we're men. And so it would follow that men must not be warm, loving, or demonstrative. To be emotionally involved with someone is a sign of weakness. It is also weak to feel or to care or to be vulnerable—in short, it is weak to be human!

Men are conditioned by our culture, by movies, television, and books, and their family and friends to accept the role of the "restricted man." The restricted man does not cry. He's always in control. He shuns intimacy—even fears it—and he can't make a close connection with anyone. But never mind all that. The point is, he's cool!

And what about a woman in our society? She grows up learning to be caring, loving, and concerned. She is allowed to show her emotions. She has the right to cry and even lose control—after all, she's the little woman. Showing emotion has been equated with weakness, instability, and, yes, even stupidity.

For centuries women have been indoctrinated by their parents and society. "You are weak and you need a man to take care of you. You haven't the ability to make important decisions. You can't survive without a man's approval, whether it's your father, husband, son, or lover."

The message goes on: "While you're surviving, you must always care for others, sacrifice your own life for your children and your husband. Remember, true happiness lies in being the opposite sex, the second sex, the inferior sex."

But here the message is paradoxical. How can you have an intimate relationship with anyone when you yourself are nothing, when you only exist in terms of another?

Both men and women play self-defeating roles, both Mr. Cool and the Little Woman, and these roles are effective barriers to intimacy. When and where do the barriers arise? How do we learn our roles? Where do we pick up our fears, our vulnerabilities and weaknesses—as well as our strengths?

Our first experiences with intimacy and love come when we are babies, and from then on our behavior is influenced by what our parents do. It's from them we learn values, discipline, our limitations and our strengths. Parents define, for the child, just who he is. Their attitudes shape his development, and, among other things, they teach him intimacy by example and practice. We shall explore just how parents either encourage or inhibit the development of intimacy in their children in Chapter 8, "Intimacy Begins with a Gentle Touch."

Three

ECP—Extra Communication Perception in Intimacy

The Message Behind the Message

Communication is an absolute necessity if we are to achieve intimacy. We think of communication in terms of talk, but we often forget that there is more to talk than words alone. Extra Communication Perception—what I call ECP—can amplify or diminish any message we send.

Take Nancy as an example. She has just met her mother-in-law for the first time, and she is uneasy and anxious. While preparing dinner, her mother-in-law says to her, "Would you mind making the salad? I never seem to get it right and Tom tells me yours is terrific."

Nancy pitches in at once, glad to be able to do something to help. She feels comfortable and realizes that soon her mother-in-law will accept her completely. She has received not only the obvious message, *You make a better salad than I do,* but also the ECP behind the words. *I am accepting you. I am going to let you become a part of the family. I respect your ability. I am not going to dominate you.* The groundwork for an intimate relationship between the two is being laid.

In this case ECP strengthened intimacy—but just as often ECP can destroy intimacy as well. Take the young couple who are driving out to the beach for a picnic on a warm June day.

As they park the car, the man gets out and looks up at the sky. He shakes his head with a frown. "It looks like rain," he remarks.

Suddenly the woman feels all the joy go out of the day. She knew he hadn't wanted to come on the picnic, but she had coaxed him into it. Still—why should she feel so let down? All he said was, "It looks like rain"—in fact it does. She knew that before he spoke—but there was a great deal behind his spoken words.

He was really saying one thing and communicating something entirely different. *"I didn't want to come on this picnic in the first place. There was a Yankee ballgame on TV that I wanted to see. You always drag me along on these stupid outings. Maybe we aren't suited to each other. I'm not so sure we should be living together."*

She could read all these messages behind the simple comment "It looks like rain." These messages were all ECP messages, the extra messages that go along with the spoken words. In a different context, he might have meant no more than what his words were saying. In the context of his reluctance to go, his words took on extra meaning.

There are many forms of ECP that can emphasize, minimize, distort, or change the words we use.

"Would you *mind* turning down the volume on your stereo?" The emphasis on *mind* makes a simple request an accusation. Mother got her point across. The ECP does not, however, explain what she is mad about. She might be mad about the room that wasn't picked up, the help missing at dinner, or that bad report from school.

"Get that dog out of here!" Father yells as he comes into the kitchen. The sheer volume of his voice tells the children that the *power* and *authority* is home. It also says, *I've had a long day at the office. I don't want to be bothered. Don't give me a hard time.*

"Mom never bought a bakery cake," a husband states, rubbing in the fact that his wife doesn't bake. He is implying that his wife isn't as much of a woman as his mother was.

"Darling, you know the two-piece look is out," a sister-in-law declares, putting down her brother's wife at a social gathering. The tone was sweet, but the ECP clearly says *You really have no taste!*

"You dampen the cloth before you put the wax on," a father lectures his teenage son who is polishing the family car. His ECP message was, *You can't even read the message on the can. You're stupid.*

Lecturing, sarcasm, putting someone down, and making comparisons—all of these negative forms of ECP are used by most people at one time or another, and most often they are directed toward someone who is emotionally close to them. Inevitably, these messages become forces that destroy relationships and intimacy.

If you don't want ECP to damage your relationship with someone else, you can control or counter the negative message with a positive one of your own. The daughter with the loud stereo can say, "I'm sorry, Mom. Will it help if I turn it down and close the door?" Her ECP message is, *I'm going to be cooperative and meet you halfway.*

The son whose father bellows about the dog being in the house can use ECP by saying, "The dog likes to be with the family, but I'll take her outside." The message behind the words? *Aren't you being unreasonable?*

The wife who's put down by her sister-in-law's comment about her dress can come back with "Clothes are not that important to me." The ECP? *This is me. I'm secure in myself. Let's meet as equals.*

The wife whose husband compares her to his mother can handle him with a little gumption. "I'm not your mother!" Her ECP adds, *and I'm just as much of a woman!*

The son, lectured by his father, can assert his own ability. "Come on, Dad. Give a guy a chance." The ECP is *I can read the directions too. Stop playing the heavy parent.*

In each case the reply, while avoiding hostility, asserts the facts without destroying intimacy.

Body Language

While we communicate with our voices, we are also communicating with our bodies. The ECP of body language is the unconscious way we tell another person what we are really feeling. It is difficult to lie in body language.

"I *am* listening, Mother!" A teenager protests as she stares up at the ceiling. Her words say one thing, her upturned eyes another. She is effectively signaling disinterest.

A lover, even as he declares his love and affection, folds his arms across his chest to signal, "I don't want to get close."

"I'm not upset or angry at you," one businessman protests to his partner, but the partner gets the message in the tightly clenched fist. "I am so annoyed that I want to hit you!"

A young wife, smiling only with her lips, her eyes

hurt and disappointed, shakes her head from side to side as she whispers, "Yes, darling, sex was good." Her husband gets both messages and feels uneasy, wondering which one is really the truth.

In each case the body unconsciously contradicts the verbal message, and each time intimacy is eroded a bit.

On the other hand ECP—communicated by tone, volume, hidden assumptions, body language—can also work to reinforce intimacy just as well as it can diminish it. It can send a message to confirm and strengthen a personal bond, just as easily as it can send a contradictory message to weaken it.

The key to understanding ECP lies in awareness. Learning the language of ECP and knowing how to use it can be the first step to an intimate relationship. It is not difficult to learn.

Start by keeping a notebook taking short descriptions of how other people communicate with you. Listen and watch for all the ECP messages. How much advice is being handed out? How much directing is going on? Listen for sarcasm, put-downs, analyzing, and moralizing. Be aware of open or hidden anger. And listen for the constant apologizer. Find patterns in the way you behave and how others act toward you.

One dramatic case of how ECP can be successfully learned is that of a young woman named Janice who followed the note-taking idea. She had never been assertive and had trouble making close relationships until she began to keep her list. What the list revealed was a roster of *I'm sorrys, I didn't mean its, and it's my faults.* After a weekend visit to her parents the list filled two pages. At work and in social situations, her list was not quite as long, but there was still a definite pattern. She found herself apologizing regularly.

Looking back, Janice realized that every time a man had broken up with her, his brushoff had been,

"You're a nice kid, but you're too sweet for me. I don't want to keep hurting you, but you make me feel so guilty."

Janice had never learned to be assertive at home. Her father, an aggressive, angry man, used physical abuse if any of his children stood up to him. Janice followed a pattern her mother had set. She complied in order to protect herself.

"Even when I did nothing wrong, I said I was sorry," Janice told me. "Then father wouldn't punish me. I was his good little girl."

In her adult life, Janice clung to the role of the compliant child. Her father would love her only if she had no will of her own, and she felt other men wanted her to behave the same way.

Armed with the awareness she gained by her list-making, she began to try to assert herself. At the office, when her boss told her she had made a mistake dating a letter, she disagreed. "I put down the date you gave me, but I'll be glad to type it over," she said quietly but firmly.

She waited, tensed against her boss's anger, but to her surprise he said, "Well, one of us was wrong, and the way things have been going, it was probably me. Send it off the way it is."

For Janice, it was one small step toward realizing that anyone could make a mistake and she didn't need approval all the time.

Her second step was to stand up to her butcher. "No, I don't want that part of the roast," she told him firmly. "It's too near the end." She was startled when he winked at her. "You're right. Not many people know a good cut these days."

To a friend who often took advantage of her willingness to do free babysitting, Janice said, "I'm sorry. I just can't make it this Saturday."

Surprised at Janice's refusal, her friend asked, "Why not?"

Jancie knew her friend took her for granted and she worried about losing the friendship if she changed the balance of their relationship, but she decided the risk was worth it. Better not this friend than one who used her. "I just can't," she answered firmly with no explanation.

The friend was annoyed, but the next time she asked, she prefaced her request with, "If you're not busy this weekend . . ."

Applying the same assertiveness to her father was much more difficult. The first time she stood up to him, he was furious. The second time, he reached over the dinner table and slapped her across the face.

That slap awoke Janice to the fact that there was no way she could communicate with her father—and that there was no point in trying. It also convinced her that it was time to leave the nest.

Janice slowly became assertive with other people, however, and as her apologies grew fewer, she found that most people responded to her in a positive fashion. Her social life picked up. She was given a promotion at the office. Someday, when she is still more sure of herself, she'll be able to move into an intimate relationship with a man.

A large part of Janice's insecurity was her body language. When she interacted with other people, her body always signaled *I am not really worthwhile. I am sorry about this—or that.* She would avoid direct eye contact, smile apologetically, and slump forward as if pulling her body into herself.

As she became more assertive, her body language changed. She consciously sought eye contact, stopped smiling every time she thought she was in the wrong and learned to sit and stand erect. She became very aware of her posture, an awareness that came from practice in front of a mirror.

Janice discovered that as she unfolded and opened up, other people responded to her and opened in turn.

The Sterile Imperative World

Janice went through life apologizing. Others, like her father, relied on imperatives to communicate. These communications are equally inappropriate for many reasons, not the least of which is that they destroy intimacy. Imperatives are orders or commands and they can be issued not only by members of families, friends, and lovers, but also by governments, television, and newspapers. Of course we all must learn to take as well as give orders, but using orders too often in imperatives can destroy relationships with those we are closest to.

To become aware of whether you behave this way, make a list of how and when you use imperatives and when other people use them with you. Notice, particularly, when imperatives are used in a marriage, in the family, and between lovers. Here are some examples:

MOTHER: "Come straight home from school."

FATHER: "For once, finish that project."

WIFE: "You've got to call your mother this Sunday!"

LOVER: "Act like a responsible person."

When you use imperatives, you fail to give the other person any option or responsibility for his actions. You are saying, "I am telling you what to do." The ECP behind your message is, *You are not smart enough, old enough, or mature enough to make decisions on your own. You are weak and I am strong!* The command or order in an imperative makes the other person feel defensive and threatened. It can effectively block intimate communication.

It is also interesting to note that the command message is very often ineffective. The other person ignores it, or becomes angry or defensive. It is much better to use a construction that conveys feeling and understanding, which will eventually lead to intimacy.

All of the commands cited above could easily be rephrased as positive messages if they were stripped of their imperatives.

MOTHER: "I would feel better if you came home first when school let out, and then went over to Mary's house."

FATHER: "I'd really like to see what that project would look like when you finish it. It has a lot of potential."

WIFE: "I think you'll feel better if you call your mother this Sunday."

LOVER: "It makes me so relaxed when you take over some responsibilities."

What has been added, once the imperatives are taken out, is feeling: how I would feel if you did such-and-such. Phrased differently, the message places responsibility on the other person and they avoid instant defensiveness.

It is often easy to think we are using a positive message when actually we aren't. Take Erica's case. She has read all the books on popular psychology, and has even taken classes on how to communicate. But every time she tries to talk to her husband, something goes wrong.

"We just can't talk," she told her therapy group one evening when I attended. "I tried using the *I feel* messages last night, and they didn't work. In fact, things got worse. He was so angry he walked out!"

"Well, what did you say? How did you use the *feeling* techniques?" a member of the group asked.

Erica laughed bitterly. "Well, first he comes home

from work and right away announces that he's going out to play poker with the boys—for the second time this week too! I tried to keep my voice down. 'George,' I said, 'I feel awful that you never want to spend time with me or the kids. I don't understand why you have to play poker more than once a week. I feel you just come home to eat and then take off.' "

There was a moment of silence, then one of the men in the group said, "I'm with George, Erica. Sorry, but I'd be angry too."

"I don't see why. I was careful to point out how I felt, not what he did."

"But listen to what you said. You didn't talk about his feelings, only your own. First you laid a guilt trip on him for not spending time with you. Then you told him in an underhanded way when he should be playing poker and when he shouldn't be. But the last pitch is the real big one. He only comes home to eat! Man, you said an awful lot in that one about your relationship."

Someone asked Erica what she was feeling when her husband walked out the door.

She had to think about that before she answered. "I don't know," she said finally. "I guess I was only concerned with what he said about going out to play poker."

"Did he say anything about the kind of day he had had?" someone asked.

"He said he'd been hassled all day at the office, and that he was starved." Erica frowned, trying to remember. "He said the driving was hectic and the freeway was jammed." She shook her head ruefully. "I guess I shouldn't have lit into him like that."

Like many people who try to communicate on an intimate level, Erica had become insensitive to the signals she was receiving. She was using the *I feel* message to disguise the imperative *You should,* and she had also picked the wrong time, place, and atmosphere to get across what she wanted to say. She used all of the right methods, but her perception never went beyond the method. Instead, she was merely using the method to avoid the reality of the situation.

Erica wanted her own way, and she felt that if she used the right words she'd get it. Instead she should have tried to understand George's point of view as well as asking George to understand hers. She couldn't accept refusal, or the fact that she couldn't and shouldn't always win. She wasn't tuned into George's feelings of weariness and harassment because she had no empathy.

George, in turn, had gotten her message, which was "I'm the only one who counts," and he reacted in an angry and defensive manner by walking out and slamming the front door.

One right way for Erica to have handled the situation would have been to wait until after dinner coffee when George was in a relaxed mood. Then she could have said, "You know, George, I think it would be great if we could spend more time together. I know how much your poker games mean to you, but I wish we could find some way to get a few quiet evenings alone."

It will take a lot of practice and a long time to build up an intimate communication between Erica and her husband. What she needs is to develop awareness of *what* she is saying, *how* she is saying it, and *when*.

There are some situations, even in intimate relationships, where you *must* put up with imperatives in others, sometimes because you decide the risk isn't worth taking. You may not want to lose a friend or upset an ill parent or lose your job. How do you cope at times like these?

First, your self-respect should be strong enough to

realize the true situation and understand what is happening. It helps to make the other person aware of what he is doing without antagonizing him. Being sensitive to the right time is important. You should wait for a time when the other person is not under pressure before you discuss his manner. Humor will often help, and so will empathy. Understanding another person's viewpoint is probably the most important coping tool of all.

Another important area where communication becomes difficult is across the generations. However, such communication can be achieved, and it was achieved by a woman in Erica's group who had trouble talking to her teenage daughter, Miranda. She came in glowing with excitement. "I can hardly believe it," she said, "but it really worked."

She explained that she hadn't wanted her daughter going out on a school night. "I remembered Erica and what we told her, and I waited until I was alone in the kitchen with my daughter. I felt I had to be honest with her about my feelings, but I tried to be open to her feelings as well. I said, 'Honey, I'd feel much better if you didn't go out tonight.'

"She started to turn away from me, and her voice got that funny edge. 'You mean I have to break my date for the movies?'

"I said, 'Well, I know how much you want to see the picture, but you've been very worried about that English Lit test you have tomorrow.'

" 'I sure am . . .' She looked at me, frowning a little, and then she suddenly smiled. 'You're right about that. I really should stay home and study. We can make that movie on Saturday night.'

"I couldn't believe my ears. She wasn't fighting me, and I wasn't fighting her. It was a very nice feeling!"

It was much more than a nice feeling. This mother and daughter moved toward intimate rapport. By listening to her daughter and expressing a positive concern without giving an order, the mother had let her daughter explore the problem and come up with a solution. She had allowed her to take responsibility for her own actions.

All of these people had problems communicating with other people. Strange as it seems, many of us can have problems communicating with ourselves as well. We give all sorts of commands and orders to ourselves, if we only stop to listen to them: I have to wash my hair today. I must get my work done by five o'clock. I've got to clean the house, make dinner, and finish the ironing or I can't go out to the club with Jack tonight.

Many people order themselves through life with such imperatives. They are so rigid and restricted that they never allow themselves any options, and this attitude carries over into their relationships with others. An overly self-disciplined or a severe person has difficulties being intimate with someone else. He has trouble letting another person know what he feels.

How can you overcome this?

By getting rid of the rigidity. Start by breaking a few rules. Try spending a week not using imperatives. Instead of saying, "I have to do the wash today," try, "I could just as easily do the wash tomorrow. Today is so nice I'll do something out of doors." It may not always be possible, but rules can often be broken.

Start listening to what you really *want* to do. If you can't think of anything else try having fun. Give yourself a treat. Do it. Get more comfortable with yourself and your own desires—but remember, you can only do this by hearing what your inner voice is telling you.

Is Anyone Out There Listening?

We are a nation of talkers geared to achieving and producing. We consider talking aggressive, while listening is considered passive. But if we are all doing the talking, who is doing the listening?

Many of us go through life without actually being listened to. In turn, we don't listen. In therapy doctors often find that after the first visit a patient will say, "You know, this is the first time anyone has ever really listened to me."

It can be a marvelous, exhilarating feeling to realize that someone is paying attention, that someone cares enough to hear what you have to say, to understand what your real feelings are.

Conversely, we all feel frustrated when no one hears us talk. Many people come to feel that it is useless to complain about the high price of food, for instance, because "Who listens?" The garbage isn't picked up for a week, but "You can't fight City Hall." In school teachers complain that the children don't learn, and the children know that teachers don't hear what the students really want to say.

A typical dialogue between lovers goes:

"You know we had a date today, Norman."

"You didn't tell me, Betsy."

"You just didn't listen."

"I didn't hear you."

"You'd hear me if you wanted to!"

A typical dialogue in the family goes:

"If I've told you once, I've told you a million times . . . (fill in the blank yourself)"

"I didn't hear you."

"You don't listen."

"Why should I?"

"Because I'm your father!"

"Well, you don't listen to me."

With dialogues like this, intimacy becomes an impossibility. Even when people do listen, they do so defensively. Early on, we learn that it is important not to be blamed. Whenever there is any possibility of blame, the rule becomes: jump in first and blame someone else before they blame you.

In this kind of "conversation" many people become so involved with preparing their alibis that they only hear the other person's first few words.

"Listen, I noticed the car had a new dent in the right bumper . . ."

"I didn't do it. You're the one who always gets tickets for . . ."

"Yeah, well I haven't driven the car since . . ."

You can imagine how much constructive communication will be gained from this conversation. Neither partner is really listening to more than the beginning of the other's sentence, and each is busy blaming the other. Perhaps the man who parked the car in a downtown parking lot is responsible, but neither one is given a chance to figure that out. When you are busy being defensive, you effectively shut out another's emotions, feelings, and ideas. You say, "I am not listening to you because you are wrong," or "I don't believe you," or "You are trying to blame me for your problem and I won't let you."

Band-Aiding

Defensive listening, as we have just seen, can effectively dampen intimacy, but so can *band-aiding* when it is used to allay anxiety. Band-aiding is that facile reassurance in which the anxious person is not allowed to express his anxiety. Like a band-aid over a scratch, you relieve him with, "It's all right."

But the relief is only a surface cover, like a band-aid. As you reassure him, your ECP says, *I don't want to deal with this problem. I don't want to be involved with your bad feelings. Let's cover it up.*

The troubled partner *knows* it's not all right. He wants you to recognize that he's frightened or upset. He needs someone to share these feelings.

Band-aiding can be recognized by expressions such as: "It's all right." "You'll feel better about it in the morning." Or, as young people say, "No sweat," or "That's cool."

Catch phrases like these fail to alleviate the anxiety of another person. In practice, they only serve to make it worse. They cut off further communication when a person really needs to be intimate and explore the real reasons for his or her anxiety. Frustration sets in.

"I hate getting up in the morning," a usually energetic older woman named Margaret tells her husband. "I'm so tired."

"So stay in bed. You don't have to get up."—Fred sticks on the first band-aid.

"It's more than tiredness."

"Maybe you need more sleep?"—The second band-aid goes in place and she senses the tenseness in his voice.

"I get this feeling of being afraid, scared."

"It's nothing. No one likes to get up in the morning."—Slap a third band-aid on and the conversation is finished.

What happened? The husband, sensing his wife's anxiety, reacts with anxiety of his own. While he attempts to bury his own fears, he dismisses hers. She, in turn, learns that he is uneasy, and she grows more fearful. If being afraid to get up in the morning is so terrible that her husband won't hear about it, then she must really be going crazy!

She pulls back, unable to explore and rationalize her own feelings to the one person she should be able to confide in.

An extremely important factor in intimacy is knowing that both partners can share not only good feelings they have about themselves but also bad ones. Let us return to the couple who failed to get to the bottom of their troubles by band-aiding and see how the husband, by active listening, can lessen his wife's anxiety.

"I hate getting up in the morning. I'm so tired," she says.

Her husband nods. "You do seem to be very tired this morning."

"It's more than tiredness . . ." She pauses and after a moment goes on. "I get this feeling of being afraid, scared."

"Scared?"

"Yes, scared. I just want to crawl under the covers and stay there."

There is a long silence, and then she goes on. "The house is so empty now that the children are gone."

"I think I know how you feel. The house has been awfully quiet since Abigail went to college."

She sighs. "Do you? I feel useless and lonely when you leave for work."

"It must be upsetting to feel that way."

"It is. I'm still young and healthy. Maybe if I got a job or did volunteer work I could feel my old self again—I've always liked being with people, helping."

This is a capsulized example of two people trying to deal with anxiety in an intimate way. When the wife first expresses her feelings, her husband responded by paraphrasing what she had said. To the wife, this was a signal that her husband was *really* listening, that he was clarifying, for himself, what she wanted to tell him. His head nod showed interest and encouragement.

"I get this feeling of being afraid, scared."

After she said *afraid*, he picked up the ECP behind

her pause, and he waited until she got out more of what she was trying to explain—not only to him, but to herself. Then he repeated the word *scared* as a question. This was further encouragement to her to continue. He was careful to hold his own feelings of anxiety in check and to concentrate on hers.

When there was a long silence, he didn't jump in with band-aiding or quick solutions. Even more important, he didn't say, "It's nothing. Forget it. You'll be okay." Or, what would be even more devastating and confirming of her worst fears, "You must be crazy. What have you got to be afraid of?"

He waited quietly, and she, knowing he had been listening to her up until then, was able to go on and explore her feelings and emotions as well as the reasons for them.

"I think I know how you feel" is an *empathy* statement. It says to the anxious person, "I can put myself in your place and understand your scared feelings."

Another *empathy* statement is, "It's very upsetting to feel that way." This isn't an *opinion-giving* or *advice-giving* statement. By recognizing his wife's feelings, the husband makes her feel less anxious and opens the way for her to handle her fears.

When you are an effective listener, you pick up a tremendous amount of information about the other person and also about yourself. As you learn to listen to people, they in turn learn to listen to you. Active listening is a learned skill. Like any other skill, it takes practice and then more practice. At first you will be unsure and awkward, but the longer you work at being an active listener the more easily and more naturally it will come to you. Here are some points to keep in mind.

Keep your voice down. Lowering your voice also lowers your irritation and makes communication easier.

Listen for pauses. Don't jump in with a phrase. Instead say "uh-huh?" or nod. Let the person who is talking get out what they want to say.

Suspend your own feelings. And your thoughts. Hear what the other person is trying to tell you. By recalling out loud what the other person says, although not parroting him, you are letting him know that you heard him.

Active listening allows you to get inside another person, to understand what he is feeling, to pick up the content of his message beyond the actual words.

Is there a risk in active listening? Of course. By using the skills we've mentioned you allow yourself to know the feelings of the other person, and you risk suspending your own feelings. The emotions you feel may be more his than yours. You are, in a sense, inside his skin.

You might think there is a risk that you will begin to think as the speaker does, losing a bit of your own identity. But you are only suspending your feelings for a short period of time. Perhaps he will convince you—perhaps he won't. At least you are giving him an honest chance.

It takes great inner strength to risk having your attitudes and opinions changed. You need great courage to be open in the face of hostile or bitter feelings. Old habits of defensiveness are hard to break, yet if you can open yourself up and allow yourself to hear another's emotions, you will be taking a big step toward greater intimacy. It is also often an act of great love and understanding. For most people it is easier to communicate a negative message than a positive one—but it is less intimate to do so.

Some of the most frightening feelings for many people to reveal are deep and loving ones especially to those who are close to them. "Well—she already knows I love her." "Any kid should know his own father cares for him." "If I didn't really like you, I wouldn't stay." These are just a few of the excuses people use to avoid saying the words that another most deeply needs to hear.

Too many people are convinced that expressing love is dangerous and leaves them open to rejection, ridicule, and embarrassment. To say, outright, "I love you," "I care about you" is an assertive act, and it is not without risk. But the risk is well worth the taking.

Four

Rediscovering You

At one time or another, all of us ask ourselves, who am I? How can I get in touch with this real self underlying all my surface behavior? How can I become myself? In the final analysis, we must all understand the totality of what we are. We alone are aware of our own experiences. We alone know what our inner feelings are and what any experience can mean to us.

But many people are not in touch with their experiences, thoughts, or feelings. In a sense they are aliens living within their own bodies. Many block out their feelings and deny their emotions. They are afraid to feel, to experience, to do their own thing. When their bodies and emotions are so foreign to them, there is no way they can become intimate with themselves.

Ask yourself the following questions and answer truthfully, trying not to think in terms of right or wrong. Allow yourself to go with your feelings.

Do you ever experience intense joy, sadness, or anger?

Think this question through carefully. It is easier for many of us to remember being unhappy as a child than it is to remember being happy. Try to remember a moment of joy, of real delight. Was it a particular Christmas, a special gift or treat, a moment of praise, a parent's arm around you? Capture that moment and savor it. Feel it.

What about sadness? Deep sadness and despair are often buried in our unconscious, but if you try you might remember a pet dying, a close friend moving away, the loss of a parent. Then move on and recall how you felt more recently when a lover deserted you or someone you trusted disappointed you. Can you recapture the feeling, or is it buried so deep inside you that it is unable to surface at all?

And anger. When was the last time you were so furiously angry that you wanted to scream and shout?

If you find that you are unable to recall these very natural emotions, then you may be shutting off your feelings, shutting out the inner you. One of the risks of becoming intimate with yourself is the fear that if you feel anything too intensely you will be vulnerable and open to hurt and disappointment. Now while this is true, it is also true that to deny any aspect of your basic emotions is to deny life itself. Sadness and joy, anger and love, despair and delight are all partners of life, along with birth and death.

Are you afraid of being alone, or are you good enough company for yourself to enjoy an evening, or even a few days, alone?

"Sure I can spend an evening alone," a recently divorced woman told me. "But I don't enjoy it. It's like telling the world I can't get a man."

She doesn't enjoy "aloneness" because she allows herself to be pushed into playing a role. She is behind the times, and if she ever discards the role of the "useless woman" she may find, like many of us, that she can be as good company to herself as she is to any man.

She might start by doing some of the things that really give her pleasure, but first she must learn her own wants and feelings. As she becomes intimate with those wants, she will increase her ability to be intimate with others.

Too often men and women are afraid of spending time alone because they equate it with being unloved and unwanted. But the truth is that aloneness allows you to explore your own feelings in depth and often to unleash deep emotions. Man may be a social animal, but he is also a private one. He needs time to be with himself, to discover and appreciate his intimate self.

Get to know yourself. One of the best ways is to spend some time alone, to put yourself in a situation where no one can interrupt your growing awareness of *you*, where you can come to understand your strong points and your limitations.

Jim did just that. Late one Thursday afternoon he walked into his boss's office and said, "I'm taking Friday off. I've had it up to here. The presentation is good and it's all wrapped up. I just have to get off by myself."

His boss looked at him in surprise. "By yourself? You mean alone?"

"Alone!" Jim said emphatically.

That weekend he drove up to the mountains, and with a backpack he hiked up a trail he remembered from his college days. It took part of the first day to put aside his tensions from the job, his girlfriend Linda's obvious hurt feelings, and all the pressures of the city. By noon he was acutely aware that his body felt different. There was an ache and pull to his leg muscles, and he felt the strain of the pack across his shoulders and the not unpleasant smell of his own sweat. He was conscious of how his skin felt when the wind touched it, and every muscle ache increased his awareness of his body. When he made it to the top of the escarpment and saw the river coiled in the valley below, he knew a feeling of exhilaration and accomplishment.

Jim was finally in touch with himself. He was in touch with every feeling within his body, and emotionally he was experiencing joy at all the beauty around him. He felt sadness too, remembering that it was ten years since he had last come up here as a college freshman.

That night, in his sleeping bag, listening to the night noises, he looked up and saw the stars flung across the sky. How long had it been since he had taken the time to really sense the night this way?

"For the first time in years I had only myself," he told Linda later. "I didn't feel lonely or uncomfortable. I felt at peace with my surroundings, at one with nature, and it was simply because I was so aware of myself. I was able to think about my life, the job, us, the pressured kind of life we lead—and I was able to reason out what I wanted, and most important of all what I felt about *me*."

Linda listened thoughtfully. "Weren't you scared up there all alone?"

"No. I loved it. Oh, I wouldn't want it for more than the few days it took me to get back in touch with myself, but for that time it was great, and now that I'm back I feel refreshed, better able to cope."

Linda, living with two other women in a small apartment, had to admit that she too had often thought about getting away. Somehow her life was always tied up with others. By nature she was gregarious, having many friends, an exciting social life, and, like Jim, a pressured job. She never seemed to have enough time, and everything had to be fitted into appointments, schedules, and dates.

The idea of going off alone intrigued her, but camping out in the wilderness was definitely not her style. Still—Jim had been changed for the better by his weekend alone. He seemed more together, more aware. She thought it through carefully, and for the first time in many months she said to herself, "All right, what would you really like to do—just for you?" The answer she came up with was pampering. She would camp out too, but unlike Jim she chose a very posh hotel in the city.

She checked into the oldest and most luxurious, but after the door closed behind the bellhop she had a moment of panic. What would she do all weekend alone? Could she go to the dining room by herself? Her first impulse was to call Jim and a few friends and have a party. Far out! But no, that was not what she really wanted. She wanted to get in touch with Linda without anyone else around.

Going into the bathroom, she ran a deep, hot tub. She threw in a handful of bubble bath and poured in some perfumed bath oil. As she lay back in the water it occurred to her that in her apartment, with her roommates' constant demands, she was always too hurried, too pressured to do anything but jump in and out of the shower. Now, as she luxuriated in the perfumed bath, she stroked her arms, feeling the skin smooth from the oil. She became aware of the shape of her breasts, the slight roundness of her stomach. Leaning back, she balanced one leg against the faucet and looked at it. "You're a beautiful leg!" she said out loud, and she laughed. "Hey, I like you—I like me!"

That night she had dinner alone in her room. She looked out over the park and sipped an after-dinner brandy. Later she curled up in bed and read a gothic mystery until the late show came on.

The next morning she had breakfast in bed. Then she made a list of all the things she would like to do. She took a bus up to the museum and spent an hour in the room with the Greek artifacts. They all bored Jim, but they really turned her on.

She had lunch in a small restaurant nearby; and in the afternoon she had her hair done and got a massage. Later she picked up a single ticket for the ballet. It felt strange going out at night by herself, but she just shrugged. "Why not? I'll take myself out on a date."

It wasn't until Sunday afternoon that she called Jim. "Hi. How would you like to meet a very nice lady for dinner? Me!"

Both Jim and Linda had a strong sense of self, but in the hassle of everyday life they had both forgotten it. Linda discovered that she was able to manage quite well on her own, and in doing so she discovered a bond of intimacy with herself.

Jim found that being alone in a different environment gave him a chance to think out various problems and feel things in a new way. Both Jim and Linda discovered a new intimacy with their bodies and their emotions—a self-intimacy.

Another question you can ask yourself and answer truthfully is, *Are you aware of what your body feels like? Can you touch yourself, even the intimate parts of yourself?*

A person experiences external reality through his body, but it is also through his body that he experiences internal reality, the knowledge of himself. We cannot become intimate with ourselves until we become intimate with our bodies.

How familiar are you with your own body? Close your eyes and visualize the color and texture of your hair. Move your fingers over your lips. Cup your hands in front of your face and smell your own breath. Push your arms up and feel the muscles in your shoulders. Open your eyes and look at your body as you move. Touch all parts of it, even the most intimate places, your penis if you are a man, your vagina, your breasts if you are a woman—what emotions are aroused when you touch yourself? Are you uneasy? Ashamed? Pleased? Proud? Get to know your own responses, to understand them. It will help you to understand your inner self and how it relates to the world.

If you are uncomfortable with your body or ashamed of touching any part of it, you are bound to have that shame affect your relationship to others. A woman who is ashamed to touch her own vagina or clitoris is going to be ashamed to let her lover touch them, and any intimacy between her and her lover will suffer.

Learn to enjoy your body. Understand it and respect it, and remember—your intimate self lives in it.

Can You Be Responsible for Yourself?

At thirty-four, a young woman I know thought she understood her responsibility to herself, but it turned out the responsibility was felt toward everyone but herself. Her life was composed of *daughterhood, motherhood, wifehood*—never *personhood*.

"All my life," she complained, "I've been what other people expected. I never understood that until I read a poem in a magazine.

Daddy's darling,
William's wife,
Billy's mother—
Where's my life?

"That poem is me! I'm thirty-four years old, and I

still don't know where I'm at. I'm nothing except in terms of my husband and my kids. Now my husband claims I'm not what he wants. I told him, 'Tell me what you want and I'll be anything you say!' "

"I don't want you to be what *I* want!" her husband exploded in exasperation. "I want you to be what *you* want."

It took a long time for her to get at the truth of this message, to realize that she didn't have to be locked into a role. She could be a mother and a wife without letting her sense of self be tied exclusively to motherhood and wifehood. When she did finally understand this, she took the first tentative step toward being responsible for herself.

She had always loved music. She had some talent, but could never find the time to play because of her "responsibilities." After thinking over what her husband said, she decided to make the time. She put aside three evenings a week to practice with a local chamber music group.

Far from being upset, her husband and children helped out around the house on those nights, and even began to boast of her performances. She said, "In the beginning I was terrified. I hadn't gone out by myself in years. I hadn't even related to other people except as a wife and mother. Now, all of a sudden, I was an individual. I'm not the greatest talent, but it's what I want to do, and I'm doing it. I found the group and got into it on my own, and I feel proud and good about that.

"It's a funny thing, but my husband and I are closer and more intimate now than we ever were. He tells me I'm a very interesting person, and I couldn't agree more."

Who Could Love a Kid Like Me?

You can't love anyone else until you can love yourself, and the same is true of intimacy. You cannot be intimate with others until you are intimate with yourself first, and one good method of becoming intimate with yourself is to take a trip back through time. Get out that old family picture album and leaf through it tenderly. If certain photos jog your memory and stir up feelings, take them out. If possible, select more than one picture, but try to find at least one that brings back happy memories, a picture with someone who said nice things about you, someone who loved you, who made you feel good as a child.

Try to find a picture of a place where you were happy, the house you lived in when you were fourteen, a stream you waded in when you visited your grandmother—anything to help recreate the pleasant feelings of childhood, to make you love that child you once were, to understand that there were lovable qualities in that child.

Steve is a case in point. He had no feeling of intimacy about himself, and he was sure that no one else could ever be intimate with him. He rationalized his own lack by saying, "Well, I'm not good looking and women go for guys with looks. Besides, I get embarrassed and feel out of place with women." Actually, Steve felt out of place with Steve.

As a child Steve had very little affection. When he was three his father left home and his mother shunted him off to relatives. By the time he was ten, his mother had made a new life for herself, and Steve was an embarrassing reminder of her earlier mistake.

How could Steve like himself if his own parents hadn't liked him? Parents, he realized, were supposed to love their children. If they didn't there had to be something wrong with him.

It was only in therapy that Steve began to explore his emotions and feelings about himself. At one point, after hearing Steve complain about his unhappy childhood, his therapist suggested that he find a picture of himself as a child and keep it in his wallet.

"Look at the picture from time to time," he said, "and try to remember what you felt like when you were that child in the picture."

"I don't need a picture to tell me that," Steve snapped. "I felt lousy. I was an ugly, stupid kid!"

"Were you?" the therapist asked.

"Christ, yes. I had ears that stuck out like plates. No one liked me."

"All right. What I'm going to suggest is a trip through time. That picture is a miniature time machine, and it's going to take you back twenty years. You can listen to what the boy in the picture is saying, tune in on what he's feeling. I want you, the grownup Steve, to understand that little boy's loneliness and sadness. Feel sorry for him if you have to, but learn to love him."

Two months later Steve talked about the picture in a session. "There's a picture of me I am still carrying around in my wallet. I was about eight years old when it was taken. That was the year my mother sent me to live with my aunt in Kansas City."

"Yes?"

"You know, I wasn't such a bad-looking little kid."

A month later Steve had taken a few more steps on the road to self-intimacy. He was getting to know that sad-faced, lonely little child in the photo. "I feel sorry for him," he admitted. "No one really cared about him. I would have liked to take care of him."

"Steve, could you love that child?"

Steve began to cry then. He wept for himself for the first time, and it was another large step towards loving and intimacy. He had learned to express his sadness and pain, to know his own feelings. In that brief moment, he had become both child and parent. In a sense, after so many lonely, troubled years he was mothering himself, saying, "I *am* lovable. I'm worthy of love. I care about me!"

Steve discovered that he couldn't be intimate with himself as long as he had no feelings about his worth as a human being. Learning to love the little child in the photograph, getting in touch with his emotions as that child—and as an adult too—was a way to increase his self-esteem.

Steve's new-found worth is so fragile a feeling that it will have to be constantly reinforced. As he becomes more aware, more secure, more worthwhile in his own eyes, he will begin to move out and make new friends—intimate ones.

Up Your Dow Jones Average

We are all capable of being loved, just as we are all capable of loving. To go a step further, we are all capable of learning to love ourselves once we discover something worth loving. It comes down to discovering something within ourselves that is valuable or precious.

One useful game-playing technique for self-discovery is to find one good trait in yourself for every bad one. Place your thoughts into stock market terminology.

Think of your emotions as if you were taking stock of them and the results were plastered on the "Big Board." When you feel low and worthless, your stock in yourself takes a nosedive. A person with a low self-stock average has trouble making intimate relationships. He doesn't believe he can be of any value to another person.

How can you get your stock in yourself to go up? Well, begin by looking at yourself differently. The congenital loser must become the congenital winner; the ready victim must become the assertive activist.

For instance, your day starts and your self-stock is way down. Your self-esteem has hit a new low. What do you do? Get into the market and start trading. Trade off your *I am dull and uninteresting* thoughts for a good aspect of your personality.

How do you make the trade? One method is by being your own stockbroker. Have a good talk with yourself.

YOU: I have a miserable personality. There's nothing good about it.

YOURSELF: Well, your sense of humor isn't half-bad.

YOU: Go on! I can't even tell a good story without lousing up the punchline.

YOURSELF: Yes, but you sure appreciate any good story that's told to you. You always get the point before anyone else. Man, you *are* sharp. Admit it!

YOU: (With grudging pride.) I do like a good joke, and you know, I think I dig any kind of humor, no matter how far out. Not many people do.

YOURSELF: That's for sure. You're fun to be with. Your friends all say that.

YOU: No one has to tell me when to laugh . . .

You see what's happened. Now keep with it. You become your own broker and build up your own stock. Compare yourself with that other guy who never gets the point of anything funny. See yourself as the guy who is sharp and quick. Add a few more winning stocks; trade in the losers. Take a risk in the market and try pushing up your average. It doesn't have to be a sense of humor. Pick any good point. Everyone has something to be proud of.

Maybe you made your kid happy when you bought him a two-wheeler and spent the weekend teaching him how to ride it. That makes you a good father. The point of it all is to invest in positive stocks and trade in the negative ones. What have you got to lose? Nothing. What have you got to win? A good feeling about yourself.

Another way to up your Dow-Jones is to zero in on one good feature of your body. In Gilbert and Sullivan's *Mikado,* Katasha, an extremely manipulative lady of the court with "a caricature of a face" brags about her "left elbow that men come miles to see." Brag a little to yourself about one of your good points. That's investing in a positive portfolio.

How are your eyes? *I have beautiful eyes. Today I'm going to wear that blue sweater that matches my eyes. It makes them look deep, deep blue.* Add a few more stocks to your investment. *My eyes are a part of me, and I am proud of them. I love to look in the mirror and see those baby blues.* Throw out the message they've been handing you about being plain. Who could be plain with such beautiful eyes? Zoom! Up goes your personal Dow-Jones.

Isn't it all just a game? Sure it is, but game-playing is a part of life—an important part. The Dow-Jones game utilizes an important psychological truism *—every one of us has some unique good qualities.* The game makes us aware of them.

Other games can make us aware of our better side. A bedroom mirror can do it. It can increase our intimate understanding of ourselves. Try standing in front of it, dressed or undressed, and talk to your reflection. Say whatever you wish, but keep it positive. This is a dialogue, but one in which your reflection can't judge you or talk back. Try some compliments.

—Hey, you look great this morning.
—What a smile!
—A suit like that looks swell on my lean build.
—Dig those breasts! Fantastic!

Remember that it's much easier to give yourself negative messages, to remember all the destructive things friends and parents have been feeding you all these years. It's a bit harder to stand up and talk out about your good aspects. You can do it by getting another dialogue going between you and yourself.

YOU: Why do I look so crummy every morning?

YOURSELF: Crummy? Are you nuts? You just need a shave. You look fine to me.

or—YOU: I've got a big mouth, just like my mother's.

YOURSELF: That's because you smile so much. You've got a great smile. Big-mouthed people are generous.

or try this—YOU: I'm so short, just like my father.

YOURSELF: You haven't an ounce of fat on you.

or else—YOU: I hate being so small breasted!

YOURSELF: How many women can go around without a bra? You really have it made with today's styles.

You can use the same technique when you're on the street. Check yourself out and give yourself approval—don't wait for someone else to give it to you. Take a few long walks and use your eyes. Notice the people around you, the green of the trees. In the city, the hot tar of the streets. In the country, the sweet scent of newly mown grass. Make yourself a part of that world. Say to yourself, *I belong here. There is no one else like me in the whole world. I am unique, a person of value. I am worth knowing.*

The Fantasy Trip

One of the best ways to build your self-esteem and to become intimate with yourself is through fantasy. In most trips through life someone else sets up the rules and regulations. Not so with fantasy. You call all the shots. The only limit is the creative free play of your imagination. You can give yourself permission to fantasize whatever you wish. There are no penalties unless you impose them yourself.

In a fantasy you can be yourself or you can change your identity. You can move forward or backward in time and manipulate other people, places, and things. You can start a fantasy and keep it going or stop it. With fantasy you can anticipate a future act and prepare yourself for it, or you can go back in time and relive a situation. This time around you can do it differently and avoid all the mistakes you made before. You can test out what it would be like to fail—or succeed.

Fantasy is often a way of testing yourself. No matter how awful the situation, nothing can really happen to you. The fantasy is yours and you are completely in charge.

Here's a test. Can you see yourself as a real winner? Try it. Imagine yourself standing on the dais in Sweden, the recipient of a Nobel Prize. You've just finished your acceptance speech, and the crowd is on its feet cheering. How does it feel? Let the emotion of success, of world acclaim wash over you. Can you accept the adulation? The admiration? Can you allow that inner self, the one that cries out for recognition, to be heard? In short, are you really comfortable with a good, positive fantasy trip?

Some people aren't. My friend Alex, a young stockbroker, wasn't. He always gave himself negative "trips." "Sure," he told me once, "I can fantasize just what it would be like if I went to a party. I'd start out meeting this really cool chick, but I know myself. I wouldn't be able to think of the right thing to say, and while I was stammering around some sharp dude would come along, and she'd take one look at him and leave me flat!"

With a little urging, Alex decided to try a positive script. He started with the kind of clothes he would wear to the party. In his old, negative fantasy he always saw himself as he was, in a conservative business suit, white shirt, neatly patterned tie—the clothes that identified him, Alex.

But there was no need for Alex to see himself that way in his fantasy. Once he understood the rules he was able to switch to French jeans, Gucci loafers, and an expensive Italian shirt. "You know, I haven't got a bad chest at all," he decided once he was into the game. "I'll leave that shirt open, almost to my belt. Maybe a gold chain around my neck. Is that too much?" When I shook my head he grinned. "What the hell. It's all make-believe!"

In his fantasy Alex stood in the doorway and looked around casually. The conversation stopped and all eyes turned to him. Now he had to fight down the feeling of panic and stay cool. Let them guess who this casual, expensively dressed man was.

Slowly he glanced around the room and he met the eye of the girl near the bar. Contact! He held her eyes a shade longer than necessary, and after a moment he walked over to her. She smiled—and—fade out. That's the end of the fantasy for now because it's as far as Alex is ready to go at this stage.

It is a mild sort of fantasy, but it isn't threatening. Alex was able to handle it. The trick, he learned, was not to fantasize to the point where it becomes overwhelming. Test each step out. Relive this fantasy a few times until you feel comfortable and relaxed in it.

Later Alex was able to continue the fantasy and carry it a bit further. He dazzled the girl with his quiet wit—he really could be witty when he didn't freeze up—and eventually it was her place or his.

Is there any value to all of this? Well, in his fantasy Alex sees himself in a completely different role and he tests that role out. Testing is the key of fantasy.

He tests his emotions, his desires, his strengths and weaknesses. True, the testing is all make-believe, but it's *his* fantasy and in a broader sense *himself* he's testing.

In practice, Alex and his positive fantasy worked out very well. It took a long time, but eventually he didn't need the loafers, jeans, and shirt to pull it off in real life. All he needed was a little self-confidence. He needed *to see himself as a winner.*

"It's really far out," he told me thoughtfully. "I even go into singles bars now, and if I see a girl who's alone and who looks interesting—why I go over and start talking to her. You know, I actually walk differently. I use that fantasy as a reference, and I find I like myself now. I don't hold myself in contempt the way I used to. If I fall back into the old embarrassment, I think about the alter-ego of my fantasy—and my confidence begins to come back.

"The other thing is, I've learned that most of the girls I meet are lonely too. But if I risk a little of myself, many of them open up and take a risk too."

I asked Alex if he looked on it all as a game. "A game?" he asked quizzically. "Well, maybe, but that negative trip I was into for so many years was a game too. It was the *no risk-no hurt* game. I felt pretty secure as long as I never risked anything. All I had to learn was that by taking a risk I could gain more than I stood to lose."

If fantasy is a game, at least it's a game that allows you to get in touch with your psychic self, to explore different and long-buried aspects of your personality. Knowing yourself, being intimate with yourself, and realizing your own worth is an ongoing process. The one risk you take in becoming an intimate and worthy person is that you give up all those negative feelings you have clung to for so many years. They were your security blanket—but all of us must throw away that old tattered blanket when we grow up. In growing up, dependency is exchanged for responsibility, failure for success, anonymity for an identity.

Psychiatrist-author Allen Wheelis wrote, "Identity is the integrity of being, and action defines a man." Action, too, defines the self. One risk doesn't mean that you have discovered intimacy; one encounter doesn't mean that you have abolished loneliness and discovered intimacy. When the action is repeated again and again it becomes a part of a man's character. Risk-taking itself eventually ceases to be a risk. The search ends because intimacy is found.

Take the risk. Allow yourself to feel, to experience, to be—yourself. Once you understand yourself, love and like yourself enough to respect yourself, then you can take the next step. You can risk being close to another person. When you have learned self-intimacy, you can take a long, careful look at sexual intimacy.

Five

Discovering Intimacy in Sex

In a popular short story, *The Most Dangerous Game,* the game is the hunting of one man by another. In human relationships, the dangerous game can be sex, and the bedroom becomes the hunting ground where it is played. Men and women believe that they are hunting for that intimate other who will give some meaning to their lives, lessen the loneliness they feel and share the joy of sexual passion. It's a sad truth that too often the hunt ends in hurt, emptiness, disappointment, and despair instead of love, fulfillment, joy, and intimacy.

Why does the hunt, and sex itself for that matter, become so disappointing to many of us? Surely sex is one of the strongest emotions a human can experience, and knowing that someone else wants us should diminish our feelings of alienation in this confusing and difficult world.

The trouble is that many of us have forgotten one important fact, that sex must be an integral part of life. We cannot divorce our sexual selves from the rest of our being. Sex is as much a part of us as hunger, love, hate, and a sense of humor. We need them all to survive.

In physical, intellectual, and emotional ways, our sexual self is affected by the world outside us and the world within. We are bombarded with sexual messages from the day we are born to the day we die, cultural messages and glandular ones.

On national television we hear educators, politicians, writers, and noted feminists declaring that woman is the sexual equal of man—but when the sponsor's message comes on we see that women are turned on by waxed floors, snow-white clothes, deodorant soap, and squeezable toilet paper. We know men aren't. Women, we're shown, are the dispensers of nurture and are concerned only with how smellproof and dirtproof their homes are.

Men, too, get a paradoxical message. The latest copy from the writer-psychologist is that men can be tender, loving, and gentle. But on the TV screen and in the neighborhood movies we see men filled with brutal violence embracing a macho philosophy.

Early on we learn to associate sex with guilt or shame, or, if we are fortunate, with love and tenderness. We watch our parents for cues. We read forbidden books and we turn to our friends for information and misinformation. It goes right to the heart of the teaching we receive from our parents. For generations young women were taught by their mothers to demand emotional commitment before they let Prince Charming into their bed. At the same time all the Prince Charmings were urged by their fathers to prove their sexuality, but to beware of getting too involved.

Girls were terrified of being *used.* Pregnancy was a sword of Damocles hanging over their heads. *Too loose, too fast, not nice* were scarlet labels waiting for the first girl to step out of line. Boys were just as terrified of *entrapment*, or worse, of having the gang discover they were still virgins!

Today we have a different sexual climate, and although many of the old cultural standards are still in effect, still being taught and believed, we are moving toward what we doggedly call the sexually liberated society. The puzzle is that there is still no lessening of sexual problems. Indeed, according to most psychologists, there seem to be more. Is this a sexual Catch 22, the more we move toward liberation the more hungup we become?

Young people today are under paradoxical pressures. Pop teen culture as well as peers are pushing for instant gratification, *casual sex.* Parents, clinging to old values, press for *lasting relationships.* Girls in college feel that there may be something wrong if they don't have sex on the first date. It's expected—in fact, it's as common as the goodnight kiss was twenty years ago—or at least this is the message young women get today. Boys know that the girls expect a sexual ploy, but instead of freeing them to enjoy casual sex, this knowledge often puts boys under more pressure than they can handle.

In spite of the macho stereotype fed to them, the plain truth is that young men do not always want only sex. In fact they usually want a lot more than the casual sex the culture suggests.

A young man at a midwestern college told me, "Sure, I can get it as often as I want, but I just can't enjoy sex like that—or even make the scene unless I really get to know the girl and like her and keep the sex going for a while. What I want is a relationship that means something—Don't laugh, but it makes a difference."

The *difference* is what intimacy is all about. While there is more casual sex around today, there is also less intimacy. The closer we come, sexually, the farther apart we grow emotionally. Twenty years ago, things were different. The balance was the other way. There was far more physical intimacy than sex. Young people spent hours in what has become a lost art—necking. All the sensual activity of cuddling, hugging, and kissing may have been frustrating, certainly there was little orgasmic satisfaction, but old-fashioned necking had a purpose. It built up an excitement and interest in sex even while it held sex off. The lovers came to know each other's bodies and each other.

It might well be a good thing to try and get the balance back. If you wish true intimacy, you mustn't settle for instant gratification. There's nothing wrong in lovers getting to know each other physically and emotionally before they know each other sexually. Casual sex, by skipping the prolonged period of physical exploration, makes the sexual act little more than a release. Gratification takes the place of warmth and sharing, and it usually ends up with two people using each other.

Alison was an example. At twenty-eight she had an unsuccessful marriage behind her, and, as she put it, "I was still a small-town girl even though I had lived in New York for eight years. I love the city, but I got so lonely. I'd go to the singles bars. I mean, why not? Most of the guys there are lonely too. I always figured that someday I'd meet a guy I could really get involved with."

But it never seemed to work out that way. There was Will she met at Maxwell's Plum. He was about her age and he had a sexy grin. They talked for an hour, trying to hear each other above the laughter and noise. They left together and walked the few blocks to Alison's apartment.

Sex was good that night, and in Will's arms all of Alison's loneliness seemed to disappear. The next morning she got up early and started breakfast. She was just putting the toast down, when Will came into the kitchen completely dressed.

"Don't bother with breakfast, doll. I have to run."

She stood there with a slice of bread in her hand, staring at him. "Last night . . ."

"Great! Fantastic!" He kissed her on the forehead, grinned, and headed for the door. "See you."

After he had gone Alison sat down at the counter. She knew he wouldn't call. He probably didn't even remember her last name. Where was the closeness, the intimacy she had felt last night? She felt used, degraded. She hurried into the bedroom and started changing the bed. Then, as she headed for the shower, she realized that if he had used her, she had also used him. Neither had been capable of anything more than a casual encounter. Once that was over she felt as lonely as before.

A week later, at a cocktail party, Alison met Patrick. He was older than she and very attractive. They spent most of the evening together, but when he suggested they leave she was hesitant.

"Come on. My place is only a few blocks away."

"Pat, let's go and have some coffee instead."

Sitting in a small coffee house nearby, Alison realized she was about to fall into the same pattern. But did she have to? Why not risk saying, "No. Let's wait." She might lose him, but what would she be losing? Another one-night stand?

When he asked the inevitable, "Your place or mine?" she said, "Look, Pat, let's cool it awhile. I like you, and I want to get to know you first."

Startled for a moment, Patrick looked at her and then smiled. "I'll buy that—in fact, I'll even buy your dinner tomorrow night. Is it a deal?"

It was, and it was the beginning of something good

and lasting for both of them. One of the reasons it went so well that first night was that Patrick was ready for something more meaningful than another casual sexual encounter. For years he had fought what he thought of as "entrapment." His own family background taught him about the hate that masquerades as love, and the desolation you can experience when that hate is gone. His mother walked out on his father when he was still a child, and in Patrick's head marriage was tied up with hurt and desolation.

Physically, Pat was a handsome, well-built young man, and he had a smooth, charming personality. In college his attitude was a cold reflection of his father's advice, "Never trust a woman."

Still, he was the envy of all his friends. "That Pat, he's on a sexual merry-go-round!" they'd say admiringly. "I wouldn't mind being in his shoes, or his bed!"

Patrick enjoyed sex, but as soon as there was the suggestion of an intimate relationship, he would drop the girl and become scarce. Emotional involvement, he told his friends, was dangerous. "A man can get hurt too easily. You're too vulnerable. The only way to treat them is to love them and leave them before they leave you."

Ten years after college, Patrick was into the singles scene. Weekends he'd be off at the resorts, and during the week he checked out the swinging bars in the city where he worked. Pat had a good job as an accountant with a toy manufacturer, and he liked his work. That part of his life made sense, but as he would tell his coworkers, he liked his freedom too.

When he finally met a woman who could offer him closeness and an end to loneliness, he tentatively broke his own long-standing rule and took a risk. After all, this woman was safe. She was married with children and had no intention of breaking up her marriage.

They had a great thing going for months—at least that was what Pat thought—when to his amazement she was the one to turn the tables and break it off.

"I don't want to see you again," she told him quietly one night.

When he asked her why, she answered bluntly, "I'm sorry, Pat, but—how can I say it? There's just nothing between us. I've tried, but you never let me close to you. We've been sleeping together for four months now, but I don't know you.

"Sure it's been good, and at first I told myself that that was enough—a good sexual relationship with no strings attached, but to tell you the truth, it's like going to bed with a robot. You're programmed for all the right moves, but—I'm sorry. You're really a lousy lover!"

It was a cruel rejection, but it was exactly what Patrick needed to snap him out of the emotional bind he was in. The next woman Patrick met was Alison, and when she suggested coffee instead of going to his place, his immediate reaction was, "I'll go back to the party and find another girl. Hell, I'm good enough in bed to get anyone I want."

And at that moment he remembered his last affair. Did he want to go on with casual affairs all his life? He looked at Alison and was suddenly aware that he did want to know her. He was willing to take a chance and see what developed.

To their surprise, Patrick and Alison found a great deal in common. They were both joggers and they loved the opera. They met that weekend to jog around the lake, and Patrick bought tickets to the Met. The jogging became a regular thing and so did the opera. Sex, when it came, was a part of the deepening intimacy between them.

Playing the Rejection Games

In adult life the fear of sexual rejection is one of the biggest barriers to a truly intimate relationship. Some people, like Patrick, assume the role of rejector to avoid being rejected themselves. Others play a take-no-chance game. Their motto? I won't wait for someone else to put me down. I'll do the job myself. Some, as a variation of this, play the most devastating game of all, *The Victim Game.* I am your victim. I am available for rejection, indeed, I expect it.

Sandra played the victim game with rejection as her first move. An attractive young copy editor, Sandra labeled herself a loser in bed. Even before she became involved with Oliver, she was sure it wouldn't work, and the first time they tried to have sex, it didn't.

"I'm sorry. I know I don't turn you on," Sandra said unhappily.

"These things happen. We're just getting to know each other," Oliver said reassuringly.

"No. It's my fault. I'm too skinny to be sexy."

"Come on, you're gonna lay a guilt trip on me."

"It's my fault," she insisted.

He shook his head. "Can't we just drop it?"

But Sandra couldn't. It wasn't her first rejection and she was sure it wouldn't be her last. Her insistence that she be rejected, that it was all her fault, finally drove Oliver away. In desperation, Sandra went to a famly friend, a psychiatrist, for help.

He listened sympathetically, then said, "I'll level with you, Sandra. I have a good idea of what's wrong, but I think therapy is too expensive for you right now. Maybe you can help yourself."

"Tell me what to do," she asked anxiously.

"You always put yourself down. Do you know why?"

"I don't do it deliberately."

"I know that, but just take a realistic look at yourself in a mirror. You're an attractive woman and you hold a responsible job. You're smart, but you don't see yourself as you are. I want you to do that, even if you have to spend a whole day in front of a mirror! Then I want you to try to remember when you first decided you weren't sexy."

It wasn't easy and it took a lot of self-searching, but eventually Sandra realized that her inadequate feelings began when her father started teasing her for being a tomboy. "What do you want with a dress? You look great in your brother's clothes."

Sighing in disappointment, her mother helped it along. "What a shame you're so flat. If only you were built like your sister." It all went with the constant messages from the magazines and movies. Big breasts are sexy.

Over and over the message of rejection was fed into her, and eventually she began to dredge up those old tapes and play them over for herself.

Once she could make the connection between the negative messages she used today with her lovers and the memory of her father's teasing, she could begin to break the pattern and see herself as she really was. She began to understand that episodes such as the one with Oliver could happen to any couple.

Why are so many of us involved in these rejection games that serve nothing but to block intimacy? Why are we so afraid to risk a little rejection, to stand up for ourselves? The truth is, we play the game and make the rules and still do not understand what we are doing or why we are doing it. We tell ourselves we feel hurt, frightened, angry, depressed, or anxious.

We identify the feeling accurately enough, but we fail to take the next step, to trace it back to its source.

Once we know why we feel the way we do, we can turn off the loser messages. This is a bit harder, but it can be done. Find something about yourself that you can admire. See yourself in a realistic light. Nobody is perfect, and indeed, perfection would be pretty tiresome. Recognize your flaws and accept them. Everyone has them.

Losers and victims tend to exaggerate and to see themselves in a negative light. Take every loser message you have fed yourself and reexamine it. Is it really true?

Nothing ever works for me. But something must. Grab hold of that and then look for more. What was the last good experience you had, no matter how small? You'll find it wasn't so long ago. With a little honest searching, you'll begin to find more and more—enough, if you look hard, to tip the balance.

When you're beleaguered by doubt, try to see yourself as your own reinforcement. Sandra, when she was troubled, got help from her family friend. But after that her own help came from within. She understood her problems and *wanted* to change.

Like Sandra, we all bring the tired old tapes of childhood to our sexual relationships. We also bring our own unique vulnerabilities. We play out childhood scripts of rejection. Old guilts and shames come to the surface and we cling to roles assigned to us years ago.

If you have trouble with sexual intimacy, try to listen to that old tape, to what you are telling yourself. Tune in on your internal dialogues. Are you translating dormant childhood rejection messages into active rejection messages of today? Are the loser messages circulating in your head before you even go out on a date, before you meet your lover or lie down in bed next to your husband or wife?

Consider a few typical loser messages.

—Nothing ever works for me.

—She'll never put up with me.

—He's only using me.

—Sure it's great, but she'll leave me. It always happens.

—He won't call tonight or tomorrow—oh God, I know he won't call!

—I know she wishes she had married someone who could give her the things she wants—and deserves.

—He only stays with me because of the kids.

Loser messages are ways of telling yourself to expect the worst. In that way you won't be disappointed. You use the messages as a shield and don't let your guard down for a moment. If you are completely open for rejection, if you always expect it, how can you be hurt when it comes? You get what you expect. You know you're a loser—so what else is new?

If you are going to change your victim-loser pattern, you must first understand what you are doing and what you gain by being a loser or a victim. Here are a few gains.

—Nobody expects too much of a loser.

—If you're a loser, you needn't expect much of yourself. You can save yourself the effort of trying.

—You may have had a victim role in your family, and this was the role in which they accepted you. Being a victim means being accepted.

—You never have to take responsibilities.

There are many other reasons people stay losers. The list is almost endless. The point is, as a loser you are your own worst enemy. You set yourself up for continuing rejection.

To change the pattern, start small. Take a little risk. Try criticizing someone you love and see if the sky falls in. Set yourself up for a rejection you can handle and then work up to bigger ones. In each case, ask yourself if the gain is worth the risk.

Those who use rejection to keep their loser status find that no matter what the gain, the loss is greater. No matter how intimate a situation they find themselves in, they carefully manage to put an irreversible distance between themselves and their partners. And yet, these losers, more than anyone else, desperately want to be loved. But love is too frightening, the risk of involvement too great.

A young married couple would lie side by side in bed, unable to sleep. Both of them wanted sex, but neither could reach out to the other. "Why should I always be the one to make the first move?" he would think resentfully.

She fought back her tears. "It's been over a week since he's touched me!"

"Let her ask first."

"It's up to the man. He should be the one to say something, to make the first move."

Both of them were unable to stretch out a loving hand, murmur a tender word. Neither could risk an intimate gesture to bridge the gap between—as narrow as a double bed, as wide as a world.

The solution, when they finally found it, was very simple. The wife's sister was the one who helped. "You reach out first," she said firmly. "That's what marriage is all about, taking a chance. The old saying isn't wrong. Nothing ventured, nothing gained."

"But he's a man. It's up to him!"

"It's up to you to ask for what you want. Don't be a fool. Risk it."

She listened to her sister and took a chance, and was never sorry for it. He responded eagerly, and eventually learned to ask for sex too. Often we fail to understand our own insensitivity to our partners. We tell ourselves, "He always acts hurt," or "She knows I love her. Why do I have to tell her?" We refuse to empathize and we let that refusal become compounded until there is no way of bridging the gap in the double bed.

Others are able to manage the sexual union, but can't seem to follow through afterward. Take the man who after intercourse rolls over and falls asleep without a word or a touch for his wife. He may rationalize that he loves her and he has shown his love in sex. What's more intimate than sex? In reality he is effectively rejecting her. If he were questioned about what he was doing he'd never see it as a rejection.

The message his wife receives is not the one he sends. "All right. I got what I wanted, and that's all I want. I can't be bothered getting close now—I'm not that involved."

It was his good luck that a close friend of his, listening to him complain about his marital troubles in the neighborhood bar one night, put his finger on the trouble. "Why don't you hold her in your arms after sex?"

"But she knows I love her."

"Look, a woman knows these things on different levels. They're not like us. Take my advice and show her you care. It will do the trick."

And it did. It was hard for him at first, but his wife's reaction was not only a surprise, but an encouragement. What started as an effort became no effort at all. It was something he too learned to welcome.

The Chinese Puzzle

There is still another intricacy to rejection, and in a way it resembles a Chinese Puzzle Box, where you open one box only to find another, and another and another. Many people are so "hooked" on rejection that they pick a partner who can be counted on, like their own father or mother, to reject them.

The man who selects a "martyr" for a wife knows that she will exhaust herself with the children, the housework, the cleaning, and errands and inevitably be too tired for sex. If he starts any sexual overtures, she is bound to reject him, and as she does she will manage to subtly blame him, to lay a guilt trip on top of his rejection. Though he may respond with surface emotions that range from annoyance to cold fury, deep down he will feel a comforting satisfaction in the way things have worked out. After all, his fears have been confirmed. He's justified in his expectations. He expected rejection and he got it.

Both men and women are adept at setting up sexual situations where rejection will be inevitable.

It is difficult to turn these internal tapes off or to shrug off our rejection by others. We fear rejection because it is a denial of our worth. A rejected person doesn't feel that he deserves love or respect. Whether he's a painter rejected by the world for his art or a lover rejected by his love, the feeling is the same and coping with the rejection is difficult.

Yet many of us do manage to cope. Any number of artists have had their work rejected in their own time and yet they have persevered and found recognition with posterity. Most people rejected by their lovers are not destroyed. They manage to go on to find someone else. The important point here is that neither the artist nor the lover is so let down by rejection that he decides never to paint again or love again. They cope because they believe in themselves. They have enough self-love to keep going.

The defeatist accepts rejection and says, "I am no good. I am not deserving. I am worthless."

The survivor looks at it from a different angle. "If

he won't have me it's because he's not ready to make a commitment." "If she won't have me it's because she's not mature enough." Or, "He needs a mother, not a wife." And so on.

If you are a defeatist, if you accept rejection as your lot, but you'd honestly like to change, then you must become aware of what you are doing. Ask yourself, why do you end a relationship just when it is becoming intimate? Why is intimacy a threat? How do you feel when someone tells you that she loves you? When was the last time you really trusted a lover? Did you ever?

Go back and read the dialogue between the couple in bed who are each unable to make a first move. Do you recognize this pattern? Do you make the first move in your sexual relationship? Sometimes? Always? Never? If you don't, why not? Are you afraid of being rejected? Do you play the waiting game simply because the fear of an intimate touch or word is too frightening?

If you are a woman, ask yourself whether you feel "used" after a sexual encounter. Do you allow yourself to be used? Or do you fight it? Or do you abet the one using you? Can you confront your partner with your own dissatisfaction either in or out of bed?

If you are a man, ask yourself, how many old messages of rejection are cluttering up your head? Do you still carry feelings of inadequacy into every sexual relationship? Can you separate the reality of the situation you are in today from the reality of years ago?

Finally, do you set yourself up for rejection? If you do, if you can examine your behavior and recognize a pattern of rejecting, then you can begin to change it. The first step is to find ways of proving to yourself that you are worthwhile. The second step is to risk rejection.

Start with simple risks. Try criticizing someone you love. Do it kindly, with a basis in fact. See how that person reacts—how you react. Does the sky fall down? Or do they accept your criticism?

Go a step further. Ask for something you'd like. Is it given to you, or are you rejected? If the rejection comes, can you accept it and shrug it off?

Here is an important point. Ask for something you know will be refused. Savor the rejection and see what it does to you. Learn to live with it.

Make your risks a bit bolder. When you're out with your lover insist you go to a certain restaurant, or you won't go out at all. Learn to be arbitrary. Take the risk and take the rejection. Consider the rejection as if it were a tangible object. Did it hurt so much? Were you able to handle that hurt?

Start with rejections you can handle. Get used to them, and then build up. The purpose? To learn to deal with rejection, and to deal with it again and again.

If you discover that you are constantly rejecting, probe for the reasons you do this. Is it something from your own background? Or are you involved with someone who forces you into this role?

This is often a very hard type of understanding to come by. If someone is forcing you into a role, you must consider why you related to him in the first place. Can it be that you enjoy the role? If you don't enjoy it, do you get something positive out of it? Does it help you cope?

Rejection can give you a sense of power, especially if by doing it you anticipate being rejected yourself. You do it to him before he can do it to you.

The box within a box within a box is uncovered slowly. The puzzle of rejection is just as slow when we try to uncover our true motives. But it is only when we discover *why* we do something that we can change *what* we do. We must look for a proper balance between what we do to others and what they do to us. The ability to give as well as to take is a sign of maturity—and a road to intimacy.

Six

Overcoming Sexual Barriers

The Fear of Letting Go

In building a sexual relationship, we often find ourselves putting up emotional blocks against the very intimacy we seek.

—If I get too close to her, she'll hurt me.

—He's so aggressive, I just feel overpowered when I'm with him.

—If I get too involved with her she'll take me over.

—I want to be myself, not just a part of him.

—She'll make me weak, dependent, less of a man.

—He'll control me.

In a passionate love affair, we move into each other's space, physically and emotionally. Our psyches and sexual selves become so closely entwined with our lover's that we fear we will lose some of our separateness, our uniqueness, that peculiar quality that makes us individual.

Physically, the sexual act requires that a woman's body be invaded and that a man allow himself to be engulfed. A loss of physical boundaries can occur, and in the heat of emotion there can be a confusion about where one person begins and the other ends.

We want to give of ourselves in sex. We want to share our deepest feelings, to free our emotions—but to risk such passion frightens us. We might lose control and let our partner see just how vulnerable we are.

Many of us are like the primitive man who is afraid of being photographed because he thinks that the camera will rob him of a part of his soul. We believe that letting go, sexually, can rob us—if not of our soul—then of our identity.

The fear of letting go is a deep-rooted one, and it involves more than just abandoning yourself to your emotions. It carries an unconscious dread that complete surrender to anyone is akin to surrendering to death. In many of our minds sex and death are closely linked—as are sex and punishment or sex and guilt. The moment of orgasm is the moment of truth, and as we approach it we also approach death and guilt and punishment.

A woman may carry an internal warning, buried so deep in the unconscious that it may never surface. The warning says that lovemaking is wrong, wrong in terms of her parents' teaching, her religion, the morality of society—it is wrong and so she must not enjoy it. "If I do enjoy it," her unconscious mind reasons, "I'll be punished for that enjoyment. Not enjoying it will make me miserable, but that must be the price I pay for what I'm doing!"

The internal warning guarantees that she will not let go, that she will deprive herself of the full joy of sex rather than take the risk of surrendering.

To men too, letting go can be tied up with guilts and fears. They do not fail at orgasm as often as women do because orgasm is physiologically easier for a man, but the guilt and fear can take over the moment after orgasm, once the compelling drive toward it is satisfied. Men can then turn off emotionally too, effectively curtailing any letting go.

The fear of letting go sexually carries over into other areas. We are afraid that marriage, living together, having an affair will somehow change who we are and what we are. We worry that we will begin to define ourselves in terms of our lover, and in terms of our commitment.

This is particularly true when one person takes over another and dominates the relationship. Then the fears become real. One thinks, *"She has taken me over,"* or *"He has control of me."*

In a sexual relationship, women are more likely than men to suppress their own needs and individuality, to become dependent, passive partners and let men dominate them. They are still replaying an old social script that reads, *A woman must be what her man wants.*

How many women have been brought up on those romantic novels where the heroine, in the last chapter, is swept off her feet by the hero? Swooning in his arms, she forgets time, place, and even who or what she is. She remembers only the myth of being possessed, of being one with her lover.

Unfortunately this myth can play havoc with an intimate relationship. It arouses too great expectations and groundless fears. The expectation? I must allow him to take me over and I will find fulfillment in his joy.

Men, raised with their own sexual myth, believe they must take over and possess a woman, dominate her, be the aggressor. . . . And yet, cutting through these expectations are the fears. On her part: *If I let go, I will lose a part of me. I will lose control.* On his: *She will take advantage of me.*

True sexual intimacy is not based on taking over or being taken over. Sex between two people should allow each one his or her own emotions, responses, fantasies, and expressions. A unit should be formed without the loss of one within the other.

In a sexual relationship that is based on love, each partner must have respect for the other. If you are afraid to risk letting your partner know what you want, need and feel, you are setting up blocks to intimacy. You must trust yourself and your partner. Intimacy is not an all-or-nothing business. It is an ongoing process, and it is deepest when you get to know your partner not only sexually, but *emotionally and intellectually*.

The Liberated Woman in Bed

Any two people can experience an intimate moment, but it takes work to build an intimate relationship, work combined with honesty, self-respect, and trust. Without trust you dare not risk letting go, and without self-respect and honesty, you can find yourself in the same bind that Sarah was in.

Sarah was afraid to let go because she had locked herself into a sexual role and her boyfriend, Ted, into another. Playing these roles, she found out, can prevent intimacy in sex.

Sarah liked to think of herself as a liberated woman. After all, she had a career and a serious boyfriend. After college she flew out to San Francisco on the promise of a position with a small publishing company, and she moved in with a girlfriend from her college days.

Within a year Sarah had moved on to become managing editor of a small trade magazine. She had her own apartment, then, and eventually had an Affair. She liked to think of it with a capital A. If her parents or her friends back home only knew—Yes, she was truly a liberated woman.

The only trouble was the affair itself—or, to be more specific, the sexual part of the affair. Sarah felt that she wanted more out of it. "I guess I enjoy sex with Ted," she told her former roommate and closest friend. "But somehow I've gotten into—well, playing a part."

When her friend asked what she meant, she tried to explain. "I always wait for him to make the first move, and I sort of go along for the ride. What bugs me is that it's only when we're making love that I'm afraid to say just what I want or how I feel. I mean, I'm not afraid to tell him how I feel about politics or where we should go for dinner or what movies I like. I can stand up for myself in all those areas, just the way I do on the job—But in bed? Forget it!"

Her friend understood what Sarah was saying. She'd been that route. "You're afraid to take the lead, to be aggressive."

"I don't always want to be the aggressive one, but I don't want to be passive all the time either. Sometimes I'd like to start things, or I'd like to make love to him, to be more active—you know. Instead I play those stupid little games, the come-on, the flirting, the teasing. There are things I'd like to try in bed, but I haven't been around much and anyway, he's the one who's supposed to know all about that stuff. I don't want him to think I'm too pushy. I want to be a real woman."

"And yet you enjoy sex with him?"

Sarah shook her head uncertainly. "Enjoy? Well, I get a lot of satisfaction out of his satisfaction. But I just know that there should be more to it. I want it to be better for me and for the two of us together. Does that make sense? God, I have these wild fantasies about making passionate love to him . . ."

"Have you ever tried telling him how you feel?"

Embarrassed, Sarah turned away. "I couldn't."

"Why not?"

"He'd think I was some kind of a kook. Men hate aggressive women."

"You really are into playing a part. For a liberated woman you still follow the same old masculine-feminine role game. Listen, take my advice. Try to level with him. Tell him you're a little afraid to say just how you feel about making love. See what his reaction is."

"But I'm really crazy about him. I don't want to turn him off."

"Take a chance. You have to risk a little in this life. You risked changing your job and that worked out. Now you have to do the same thing with Ted."

Sarah thought it over for a few days and finally came to a decision. Later that week she told Ted, "I want you to do something, but it scares me to talk about it."

"Try me."

"I don't want to risk hurting our relationship, but do you think that a woman—could—well, sometimes I have these fantasies about making love to you while you lean back and enjoy it!"

"Oh wow!" To her surprise and delight Ted's reaction was positive. "I've got to admit," he told her, "that I've often wished you weren't so—passive, you know?" He laughed. "Hey, I've got my own fantasies!"

"Honest? Can you tell me?"

He colored a bit. "Aw, Sarah—I'm ashamed to. A nice girl like you . . ."

Nice girl-bad boy! Sarah began to understand that Ted too had been playing a role. "I trusted you," she said. "Now trust me."

"Have you ever heard of oral sex?"

"Of course! What do you think I am?"

"Well?"

"Okay. Let's try it."

Listening to Ted, Sarah felt herself becoming excited. Sex that night was better than it had ever been. Afterward, lying in each other's arms, they exchanged even more intimate secrets.

"What happened," she told her friend later, "was like a breath of fresh air. Before, it was just an affair, a sexual adventure. But now we're beginning to know each other and trust each other. Do you know—we're becoming intimate!"

The intimacy that came to Sarah and Ted was based not only on trust in each other, but on the fact that both were challenging the old stereotyped roles that equated sexual aggression with masculinity and sexual passivity with femininity. Both of them were role-bound, but once they began to question their roles, they were on the way to breaking out of them.

Sex becomes not only more exciting, but also more intimate when we refuse to be bound by rigidity of habit or by cultural stereotypes. It is in an atmosphere of trust, mutual caring, and understanding that sexual partners become free to explore what is best for each other and what is truly gratifying in this most intimate of all relationships.

There must be a reciprocity, an exchange of both positive and negative feelings, and each partner should be free to talk about vulnerabilities as well as strengths. When Sarah said to Ted, "I want to tell you something, but it scares me to talk about it," she was really letting him know that she was vulnerable. Exposing your vulnerability takes a lot of courage and trust. Later, when Ted said, "I'm ashamed," it became an exchange of vulnerabilities, a reciprocal act of trust.

When you take a chance with intimacy, you must be aware of how the other person reacts. Is he sensitive to your feelings, or does he immediately defend himself and attack you? Does he turn off, or turn away?

Sarah and Ted each took a risk, and it worked out.

But sex is a highly personalized area. If Ted had drawn back, Sarah would have been faced with a difficult choice—to go on as they were, or to break off the relationship. Before we take a risk, we should be aware of the consequences, but we should also understand how important it is to gain what we're after.

Try risking small things first, and test your partner's reaction. Each risk is a step toward a deeper relationship. If the steps are small, and you are sensitive to your lover's reaction, you don't face the danger of spoiling the relationship.

Role Playing

A woman may risk success in the business world, but there is no guarantee that she will also risk it in the sexual world. In fact, many successful career women are convinced that they have lost their femininity by competing with men. These are women who live independent and responsible lives, yet resort to role playing in sex. As resourceful as they are on the job, they still become childish, teasing pussycats in the bedroom. They are afraid to express their own needs, desires, and fantasies, afraid of the label of *unfeminine* where it counts most—in sex.

Ted, like Sarah, was able to accept the change in their relationship and examine his own role playing. In that respect he was a very unusual young man. Most men are not like Ted. They feel threatened when women begin to assert themselves. They like the old status quo where they can call the shots, and they are not willing to risk change. And why should they? Aren't there plenty of young, pretty girls who will accept them on their own terms?

Other men think they have accepted assertiveness

in women until they become involved in a sexual situation. Dave, for example, tells his close friend, "I met this great chick at a party last night. The minute I walked into the room she began to come on to me. I mean, she moved right in. Now I don't mind that. Why shouldn't a girl make the first move?" His voice dropped. "Would you believe she tried to tell me what to do later when we went over to my place? She told *me* how to make love to *her*!"

"You're kidding!"

"As if I didn't know what to do. I ask you, what kind of chick acts like that?"

His friend shook his head. "I'm with you. I can't take a woman who wants to take over and act like a guy. So what happened?"

A bit bewildered, Dave confessed, "Nothing. I just couldn't make the scene. I've balled a lot of chicks in my time. I told her that. I know what to do. No girl ever had to tell me before."

Dave was all gung-ho when the girl came on to him. He could take that much assertion, but once between the sheets he panicked when she wouldn't follow the rules.

Many of us are like Dave. We talk a good game of liberation, but we still cling to the old roles. We're afraid to drop our masks and reveal ourselves to our lovers.

Where did all the role playing start? Was it bred into us? Or is it something we learn as children?

Psychologists doubt that our roles are genetic. In all likelihood they start when we're children. A mother scolds her young daughter. "You're not being ladylike. Little girls don't act like that."

The scolding stays with the child and it's constantly reinforced by other lessons.

—Here's a doll and toy dishes to play house.

—Now don't act too smart with the boys. Let them think they know more. No boy likes a clever girl.

—Remember, you can catch more bees with honey. Smile.

Even Dad gets into the act. He praises his baby girl. "Only three and already she's a flirt, a real little sexpot!"

Later he tells her, "You'll never have to worry with a pretty face like that."

The boy gets different, but equally strong messages. From his mother he hears, "Just like a boy. Always dirty and into something." But it is said with a touch of pride even while she complains. "I just can't handle you. You're too much for me."

Dad also helps with the programming. "Don't come crying to me. Boys have to learn to fight their own battles," or "No son of mine is going to act like a sissy."

As he grows older, the messages continue. "Be a man. Get out there and make it. Don't worry about the girls—you can have your pick."

Growing up, the boy and girl replay the messages and accept the roles. How else can they get approval? *Be a good girl*, Mother said, and she interprets good girl as a gentle, accommodating woman. The boy grows up convinced that he has to be strong. He mustn't show emotions. Girls are there for him to pick and choose.

It isn't surprising that in the sexual bed the men and women retreat into the roles of *strong boy* and *good girl.* No matter how they function in the outside world, as the clothes come off the masks go on. The role playing begins and each partner, hearing the old tapes play, tries to live up to the expected role.

In spite of this, men can be just as sensitive as women. They can be passive in a love affair as well as active, sensitive as well as blunt, and they can enjoy gentleness as much as women do.

Role playing in sex does not allow the partners to

know each other fully or to explore their physical and emotional potentials. In a long-term relationship, such as marriage, role playing eventually leads to frustration and anxiety as husband and wife conspire to preserve a facade of false intimacy. Without an honest exchange of feeling, sex becomes dull and routine and sometimes just dries up.

In their search for an intimate relationship, many people fall into the masculine-feminine role-playing games. Are you one of them? Here is a quick, off-the-cuff way to alert yourself to how deeply you believe in our cultural myths, to how much of a mask you wear.

The following list of adjectives describe human attributes. Read them through, and if one suggests masculinity put an M after it. If it suggests femininity, put an F after it. Don't think about the words. Rely completely on impulse and intuition.

1. Strong
2. Active
3. Gentle
4. Aggressive
5. Sensitive
6. Authoritative
7. Nurturing
8. Wise
9. Warm
10. Sexual
11. Sexy
12. Caring
13. Emotional

If you put an F after 3,5,7,9,11,12, and 13, then you are probably into role playing. You have accepted the cultural myths of what makes a masculine or feminine person. Try putting an F *and* an M after each word. Try out the concept of a gentle man, a wise woman, a sexy man, a strong, authoritative woman, a nurturing, emotional man. Think about those descriptions for a while and you'll see that they fit, for all emotions are a part of the human makeup, and to generalize about either sex is to create a set of rigid roles.

A Warning! Don't Take Off the Mask

Is it ever possible to stop all role playing, to unmask ourselves completely, to drop all pretense, to say to our intimates, "This is truly me. This is how I really feel. This is what I want. This is what I need."

It isn't possible, because to do so would leave us unable to cope with many of life's situations. It would violate our deepest sense of privacy and probably would destroy those we care about most. While much of our role playing and masking is harmful to intimacy, some degree of masking is always essential.

We learn about masking very early in life. The child is expected to be polite to his elders. He must smile and be civil to Grandma, even if he is annoyed that she has taken him away from his play. Showing what he really feels would hurt or upset her. By masking his feelings, he learns several valuable lessons, not only in coping but in human behavior.

He learns that adults approve of polite children, that masking his real feelings can keep him from hurting someone he loves—indeed, can make a loved one feel better.

The teenager becomes a master at masking. It's his best way of managing all the bewildering new emotions and feelings generated by the flood of hormones running through his body. Caught on the edge between child and adult, dependence and independence, and filled with sexual desires and fears, teenagers hide behind many masks to protect themselves.

We are all familiar with the expressionless face, the *cool* attitude, the leave-me-alone shrug of the teenager. We remember, from our own adolescence, how often we could deal with our parents only by hiding behind one of those masks. Many of us see our children using the same gestures, the same masks to hide from us. The teenager knows that to reveal, even to himself, the mixed bag of emotions within him will leave him open for more hurt, misunderstanding, and guilt than he can handle—and so he copes by masking.

And as adults we use masking every day of our lives. None of us are secure or free enough to reveal all our inner feelings to everybody. It would be too uncomfortable, chaotic—even dangerous.

For example, we are jostled in the subway and feel a quick rush of hostility, an urge to hit back. We mask it. Our boss is annoyed. We mask our anxiety and assume a confident air. A little girl mispronounces a word. It's funny, but to laugh would hurt her feelings, so we mask again. There are hundreds of ways we mask every day. It's all a part of learning to live together.

But surely we can be open and honest with those we love? Not always. Consider the case of a close friend who recently lost his job. For over a week, he told me, he masked his anxiety and fear from his wife. She was about to leave for Europe on a conference, her first trip there. To be honest with her would have ruined her trip.

In turn, seeing through his mask, but dimly, she sensed his anxiety and kept reassuring him that she would be all right. Both were concerned for each other, and when she returned and discovered the truth, she felt neither betrayed, angry, nor hurt.

"We know each other so well," she told me. "He realized that I wouldn't leave at a time like that, but he cared enough for me and knew how important to me it was to go. He hid his own feelings, and I think that's love, real love!"

If you care about someone deeply, then you should know when to put on the masks and when to take them off. Dropping all roles, unleashing all emotions can be honest, yes, but it can also be selfish, cruel, and destructive. No matter how intimate a relationship we have, all of us need to keep a core of inner privacy, some secret garden of self that belongs exclusively to us alone.

Accentuating the Positive

Life teaches us when to mask and when to unmask, when playing a role will strengthen intimacy, and when it will keep us from intimacy. We also learn that during sex we are at our most vulnerable. To communicate on an intimate level, we must be fully aware that we are moving into a sensitive area for ourself and our partner. Timing, delicacy, and sensitivity are all needed.

How can you start sexual communication without hurting your partner? How can you unmask without being hurt? One way is to accentuate the positive rather than the negative. It is always less of a threat when you reinforce what is good about your partner, your sex together, and your feelings for each other, rather than starting off with what is wrong about it.

Take, for example, two people who are lying in bed after sex. He feels that although they care about each other, the physical part of their lovemaking is not as free nor as exciting as he wants it to be. How can he tell her this without criticizing her or hurting her? He looks for something positive.

He: What I love about you is your warmth. You know, you're a very giving person.

She: I want to be like that when I'm with you. (She hesitates.) But I feel a little embarrassed about it.

He: But I love it when you hold me like this. (Showing her.) It really turns me on. It's a great feeling.

She: I want to do it, but I'm a little shy about it.

He: Maybe we can work on your shyness together.

This couple, new in their sexual relationship, are beginning to communicate in an intimate way. The man, sensitive to the woman's shyness, but wanting her to touch and stroke him while they are making love, uses a combination of masking and unmasking to make it easier for her. He doesn't come out bluntly and tell her what he wants. To do that would be to ignore her sexual shyness, to leave her open to hurt, and to lower her self-esteem.

When she tells him she is embarrassed, he is reassuring, and she receives a good message about herself. It makes it easier to accept what he is really saying. "I want you to hold me and touch me more."

The groundwork for honest communication has been laid. In suggesting they work on her shyness together, he is asking for an intimate collaboration.

Sometimes this collaboration is very serious, but sometimes it can work just as well on a humorous level. Humor and fun are great levelers in sex. They can take away that therapeutic, plodding approach and put a little joy into the act.

I know one couple, two very serious and intense people, whose biggest problem was undressing in front of each other. They solved it on their honeymoon when they stayed at a Japanese hotel in San Francisco. They bathed together in the room's Japanese tub, a tub large and deep enough for two.

The laughter and fun of that experience defused their sense of shame and freed them to come together on a more intimate sexual level. The timing was right. If either had tried to discuss the problem before, during, or after sex it might have been a disaster. In the fun of sharing the tub they entered into an intimate collaboration, supportive of each other and, most important of all, they were able to laugh together, sharing the humor of the moment.

In such an atmosphere, unmasking becomes less threatening, and so does letting go. Humor is a great way to bring any situation down to normal proportions. After all, sex can exist on many levels, and each sexual experience can be different. One may be wild and exciting, another can move us to tears, and still another can be fun and games.

All too often we forget that sex should be fun and games, and why not?

Winner-Loser Games

The fun does go out of sex fast when the players, consciously or unconsciously, try to hurt, manipulate, or frustrate each other. Teasing can then turn vicious, humor can become cruel, and labeling used as a destructive weapon.

You say to your lover, "Come on, you don't think I really meant what I said?" and guiltily you say to yourself, "What is he so damned touchy about?" knowing deep inside that you really did mean it.

Some game players cleverly manage to camouflage their words and actions. They always seem to have an out, even if it means accusing the other of "imagining things." Other game players deliberately use assaultive behavior and find enjoyment in openly hurting their partners.

Assaultive behavior in a marriage is nothing new. We are all familiar with the battered wife, but how many of us can draw the line between assault and "malicious fun"?

A husband and wife are making love and he begins to tickle her. She starts laughing, then, gasping for breath and twisting away from him, she begs him to stop. He keeps on until she is in tears. Later, defensively, he says, "But I was just kidding around, honey."

"You know I can't stand being tickled."

"How did it hurt you? A little tickling? For Christ's sake, be a sport!"

She has no answer but tears.

This husband's game may not be a calculated assault, but it is certainly malicious. He knew when he started tickling her that he would drive her to the brink of hysteria. It was a "power ploy" and he had his way. He was just "kidding around." But with his "kidding" he has effectively closed the door on intimacy.

How can the door be opened? Is it possible for such behavior to be changed? In this case, if there is to be change, it is up to the wife to decide what she must do, how much she is willing to risk, to stay married. Is it worth going on like this? Does she have any choice?

But we all do have choices on every level. The wife can stay in the marriage and allow the tickling to continue, or she can choose to get out of the marriage. A third, and often effective, choice is to confront her husband. If she decides on this, she should not wait until they have sex again, but should have it out with him at a time when sex is not possible. Her position will be stronger.

She should state her feelings directly. "I don't want you to tickle me. It's cruel and you are deliberately hurting me."

HE: Hurt you? But you were laughing.

SHE: I was laughing with pain. Don't you understand that it's painful when you do that?

HE: But I wasn't trying to hurt you.

SHE: But you did hurt me and it wasn't the first time.

She has taken a risk, and at this point the husband too has his choices, depending on how much he truly loves her. He can decide to try to change—and his wife would certainly go along with him—or he could continue his hostile action and refuse to change. Then she must decide. Should she stay in the marriage or get out of it? The third possibility is that he could refuse to recognize his problem, and then her choice again is to stay or go.

The choices are many, but not endless, and often, if one partner states clearly, "I would rather we tried to work our problems out, to find out why we hurt each other, because perhaps I'm hurting you too—" a husband will meet a wife halfway. At least it is a long step away from game playing.

Physical and near-physical assault are men's games. Women have theirs as well. A woman who feels hostile to her lover may resort to a sexual put-down. She plays her game in bed. When he touches her breast, she says, "I suppose that's a come-on?"

"I thought you wanted to make love tonight?"

"Not if you can't do better than last time."

"What's that supposed to mean?"

"You never learn, do you?"

Her attack has been carefully built up, and it becomes a cruel, sexual assault on her lover. She, in leading up to it, and he, in going along with it, are playing a deadly game that effectively cuts off any chance of intimacy in or out of bed. In fact, they collaborate in destroying intimacy.

Gentle, loving teasing can be a fun game, but push teasing or give it a little twist and it becomes cruelty.

"Next time around I'm going to pick a woman with a little meat on her," he says sarcastically.

"What a mean thing to say!"

"Hey, babe! I was only teasing." Teasing, yes. But he's also hiding behind the teasing to get his own back at her.

When men play games, in and out of sex, they tend to concern themselves with power. Because of their position in society, women use manipulation more often in their games. Robin is a game player, and manipulation is the name of her game.

In bed she jockeys for control of the situation. Her husband, Bill, wants sex, and she agrees. But after a moment he feels her wince.

"What's wrong?"

"My head."

"Damn! Why didn't you say so before we started?"

"I didn't want to upset you."

"I guess you think this doesn't upset me. What am I supposed to do? Pack it in ice?"

Bravely Robin answers, "We can do it if you really want to. I don't want you to suffer, Bill, just because I have a headache."

"Forget it!" Bill says furiously. "Damn it!"

Tears begin to roll down her cheeks and in a small voice she pleads, "I can't help it, Bill—really I can't!"

Realization of his own insensitivity calms Bill down. "Okay, honey. I'm sorry. I guess I overreacted."

"No, it's all my fault." Now Robin takes charge of the situation. She has manipulated Bill into a powerless position, and power is what it's all about. Men know they have the power. Women, to get it, sometimes feel that they must turn to subtler maneuvers. Robin's headache is a classic power play.

Robin used sex to play on Bill's guilt. Very often other women use sex for getting material things, gifts, better jobs, prestige. But the sex offered under this contract, in and out of marriage, is shallow and two-dimensional. The third dimension, intimacy, is always lacking. In order to have complete control of the situation, a women must separate sex from love and emotion.

Some women can do this because they are often convinced that they can live well without love. A mother tells her daughter, "You can be as happy with a rich man as with a poor one—happier even!"

Sex, in this situation, becomes a commodity, something to buy and sell. The woman sells, the man buys, and both are victims of the system.

For this ploy to be successful, women must learn to use sex as a manipulative tool. The catch is, this use of sex dehumanizes both herself and her partner. It also dictates the type of man the manipulating woman looks for.

When I was young, we used to sit around the college dormitory at night talking about love and sex and what we planned to do with our lives. The oldest and wisest among us would sum things up. "The trick is to marry an older man, not too good looking. Someone who wants you more than you want him. That's the kind of guy you can wrap around your finger."

"And what about love?"

"Love? Forget it. You can't live on love."

For the younger woman, not yet ready to settle down, the art of manipulation by sexual teasing was given our guide's approval. Sexual teasing can be a powerful game, but it can be self-destructive too. Some women who play it enjoy it so much that they avoid the conclusion—marriage. Others keep playing the game after marriage, at parties and social affairs with the safety of their own husband behind them. The game grows complex because the husband of such a woman often enjoys the effect the game playing has on other men. It gives him a sense of power too.

Manipulative games, such as these, sell a man short as a human being. They are debasing and humiliating, and actually reduce men to the status of sex objects.

When either partner is manipulated into being a sex object or less of a human being, intimacy becomes impossible. For true intimacy you need sharing and trust and respect, qualities not possible between such unequal partners.

The other deadly result of manipulation is a two-edged type of anger. The victim must bury the anger he feels—his guilt doesn't allow him to express it. Yet all of these not-much-fun games are based on suppressed anger, or camouflaged anger. All of us, at one time or another, feel anger and we all learn to live with it. Some of us can handle it and express it without losing control. Others feel they must disguise it or mask it, and still others deny it and bury it.

In the next chapter we'll see what happens to anger when it isn't handled properly.

Seven

Intimacy and Anger

Hostility

Anger is such a powerful emotion that, like love, it can sometimes frighten us. A part of being human is to be angry at times, and when two humans are involved in an intimate sexual relationship, there are bound to be moments of anger. As adults, we tend to shy away from such strong feelings, to keep intense emotions under excessive wraps. The childhood lessons were well learned. *It's not nice to get mad. People who act like that have no self-control. Don't you dare yell! Don't make me angry, or I'll do something terrible. Don't stamp your foot at me.* And, to top it all off, *Mommy and Daddy won't love you anymore.*

The adult woman says to her angry lover, "You're acting like a child." To act like a child, she implies, is to be angry and to be less of a man. With one phrase she cuts off his sexuality by threatening his masculinity.

Or a husband calmly tells his furious wife, "You

must be out of your mind. Anyone who loses control and yells like that should see a psychiatrist." To yell, to give vent to anger, is equated with loss of control. With a few choice words he accuses her of being neurotic—perhaps psychotic.

Yet most of us during the course of a normal day feel some degree of anger, and often it is directed against those who are closest to us because of their proximity and also because we feel the strongest emotions toward them. Curiously enough, a lot of anger generated outside the bedroom is held back and expressed sexually.

The Anger Bankers

The ways we express anger in a sexual relationship and the way we handle the angry feelings directed against us are often keys to how close we can be to another person. Someone always on the edge of anger cannot be an intimate person. When sex and anger are so entwined that they are difficult to separate—watch out. On the other hand, to suppress anger, to store it up and turn it inward, can hurt you—and it can hurt your intimate other.

For instance, take forty-year-old Beth, who lives a double life. During the day she is very like the Beth of *Little Women*, the Beth her mother named her for. Sweet and gentle. Her friends and her family all agree that she is the calm one. She never gets mad.

Beth follows a pattern laid down for her since childhood. *Mommy and Daddy don't love little girls who lose their tempers.* The trouble is that she has now substituted her husband for *Mommy and Daddy*. *Don't get angry or he won't love you*, is a tape that plays over and over in her mind. All day she conceals her anger, but at night in bed she lies next to

Chip with all that anger seething inside her. Beth is an *anger banker*.

What start as petty annoyances grow and grow, day after day, week after week, year after year. "I'm always tired," Beth complains, and she is. She's also depressed because her anger depletes her. At night, in bed, she can't sleep. Her whole body begins to react to her suppressed anger. Her heart pounds, her stomach cramps, and her blood pressure goes up. Beth is an angry woman who has placed herself under extraordinary stress, both emotionally and physically.

Complaints stockpile in her mind. "Today Chip didn't take the garbage out before going to work. Last week he was late picking up little Sally at the dentist. A month ago was my birthday, and he forgot that too. Eight years ago, right after we were married, he broke my favorite china tea pot—and that was in the family for years!"

Chip, lying next to her but unaware of the unreeling anger tape, reaches out to touch her. She moves away and he asks her if anything is wrong. In the dark, Beth shakes her head but doesn't answer. Chip rolls away and tells himself bitterly, "If she feels like that, to hell with her!" He interprets these constant withdrawn silences as rejection. He too is banking his grievances, and eventually he'll get back at Beth by sleeping with other women.

Beth has operated on the theory that to show anger is to open yourself up to rejection. Out of the bedroom, both pretend to be close, but at night they lie side by side in their double bed, nonintimate strangers.

Too frightened to confront Chip outside the bedroom, sweet, gentle Beth withholds sex, her only weapon in the fight.

How could Beth discharge her anger without alienating Chip? How could she release the pressure valve of her building tension? Let's play the script another way. Let's give Beth a chance to get it off her chest and see what happens.

The scene is early morning, a rather hassled morning for Beth, and to top it off Chip, on his way to work, has forgotten to take the heavy garbage cans out. Beth comes to the back door as he's backing the car out of the garage.

"Damn it, Chip, wait a minute!"

He rolls the car window down. "What's the matter?"

"You forgot to take the garbage out again!"

"Big deal, I forgot. Why are you so teed off?"

"It's the second time this week. You know I can't lift those cans."

Recognizing the truth, Chip admits he forgot. "I'm sorry."

"You're always forgetting things. You forgot Sally's appointment last week too." At this point Beth is taking unfair advantage. She brings extraneous material into the argument.

Chip refuses to accept this criticism. "Come on, that's not fair. So I forgot the garbage. I was wrong, but don't try to dump everything else on me."

Hesitantly, Beth says, "Okay, so I'll just yell at you for the garbage."

He grins at that. Then, imitating his daughter's whine, says, "You're picking on me."

They both see how silly the exchange has become, and they start to laugh. The argument ends with a good feeling and at the same time the anger in Beth has been defused. She got her feelings out *when* the incident occurred. Chip tried to defend himself, but realizing that Beth was right about the garbage, he accepted that complaint, but refused to take any generalized criticism.

In turn he expressed his annoyance at Beth. She

questioned his anger and it ended with a joke and a grin—an effective way of apologizing for the anger without losing face. Lovers must learn to communicate their hostility directly in words *when and where the hostility is aroused* instead of storing it up to use in the bedroom.

Sex does *not* have to enter fights about nonsexual matters. Have it out then and there instead of banking it all for that rainy day—or night.

Jack had a different way of banking anger and misusing it. He would save up his sexual anger and then use it as ammunition the morning after. He'd shape it into bullets and fire them at his girlfriend, Amy.

"God, this stuff tastes bitter! Why can't you make a decent cup of coffee?" or "Damnit, the toast is burned again!" and on his way out, "Don't call me at the office again. If I want to talk to you I'll call."

Only last night he and Amy had made passionate and exciting love, and now here he is the next morning, hasty and mean, out to pick a fight.

The first time it happened, Amy was stunned. But when he gave a repeat performance each morning after sex, she began to see a pattern. Six months later she told Jack that she wanted to split.

"Why?" he asked, bewildered. "Don't I satisfy you?"

"Satisfy? There has to be more to a relationship than physical satisfaction—for me anyway. I don't understand you, Jack. We have this great sex and you're warm and loving and passionate, but the next morning you're furious with me. You go out of your way to pick a fight. It always happens. What is it? Are you afraid of me? Am I some sort of witch?"

Amy had part of the answer. Jack was afraid. But he was less afraid of her than he was of himself. In those wonderful moments in bed he was able to let go, to enjoy the full spectrum of his feelings. He gave of himself and he let Amy give to him.

It was only the next morning that the bad vibes began. He told himself that Amy was too demanding. She was trying to take him over, to bewitch him. She was moving in and breaking down the wall of isolation that he had constructed, and—terror of terrors—she was forcing him to *feel*!

The truth was, Jack was terrified of intimacy, and he used anger to avoid it. In therapy he found that sex, intimacy, and pleasure were all confused in his mind with sexual guilt. With Jack it went back to a rigid, religious background. Sex meant rejecting his parents' values, but even deeper was his conviction that he had no right to joy, to love, and most important of all, to deep, pleasurable sex.

When Jack came home from work one evening and found Amy packing to leave, he was so shaken up that he promised to do something about his sexual anger. That *something* was to join a therapy group, and there he became aware of why he acted the way he did.

Awareness was his first step, and relating it to Amy and the other women he had broken up with was the second step. If he hadn't had Amy to help him he might never have made it. During the second week of therapy, the two went off for a week's vacation. It started perfectly, but ended in the old sexual hostility. But this time Amy stopped Jack at the very beginning of his act.

Having breakfast in the hotel restaurant, Jack was quiet and withdrawn. "What's wrong?" Amy asked.

"Everything!" he snapped. "Must you wear that halter to breakfast?"

Amy put her fork down slowly and said, "Do you know what you're doing?"

"Yes. I'm annoyed with you."

"No, Jack. You're annoyed with yourself. Remember what you told me about your problem."

Almost sullenly, not meeting her eye, he asked, "What?"

"You're attacking me because you feel guilty about last night."

There was a long silence as they ate, and then Jack looked up with a rueful smile. "You know something—and this is the hardest thing I've ever had to say—you're perfectly right. I'm an idiot. Pass the jam."

"But an honest idiot?" Amy smiled.

That was the breakthrough that helped Jack go on to a deeper understanding of his own reactions, and a truer intimacy.

Can this Marriage Be Saved?

Beth and Jack banked their anger—Wanda was afraid of hers. She solved every angry argument with her husband by coming on to him sexually. "Sex is always better after a fight. Making up is such fun," was how she justified herself.

What Wanda meant was, *I am so afraid when we get angry that the only way I can handle it is with my body.*

But it wasn't really sex that Wanda wanted at this point. It was reassurance. She wanted to know that Peter, her husband, still loved her. To show anger or to have it directed at her was a sign that she wasn't lovable—at least that's what she thought. So she pushed the panic button and out came her defense—sex.

Peter went right along with his wife. He'd put aside any disagreement and fall into bed instead. Afterward they'd reassure each other that all was ginger-peachy between them. They were madly in love. They were an ideal, intimate couple—forgetting that their anger was not resolved, only put aside.

Sometimes the simulated intimacy of sex lasted for a whole day or even a week, but as the same problems cropped up between them, their intimacy began to fall apart. The old arguments were warmed over and served up again, and at once Wanda went back into her sexual act.

Their relationship grew shakier as their love-making became more frantic. Neither one was quite sure what was happening, but they both knew that their marriage was headed for trouble.

Can this marriage be saved? When both partners are truly willing, most marriages can be salvaged. Wanda and Peter wanted to stay together. Peter suggested that they try a weekend at a marriage marathon that their church was sponsoring.

"Just to see what it's like," he told Wanda. "Not that we really need it—that much—but it might be interesting."

Wanda agreed. They were both still pretending that there was nothing seriously wrong.

I met Wanda through the pastor of her church several months later, and by then she was more than willing to talk to me, to tell me how she and Peter were working out their problems. "Our biggest one is anger, and I'm still working on that," she said.

"At the marathon we were with five other couples in this beautiful lodge in the woods. It was two hours from Seattle and on the drive up the two of us kept laughing at what a ball we'd have listening in on other people's problems. Actually, we were both scared stiff!

"That first afternoon Peter and I just sat there, neither of us opening our mouth. Some of what was going on was real heavy. One couple was slugging it out, the wife calling the husband all sorts of names until I just blurted out, 'Fight fair!'

"Later, Peter told me that I had interfered, and he was furious with me. We started to get into a real fight before bedtime. I couldn't wait to get into bed, and then I turned to him, ready to caress him the way I always did, but all of a sudden I drew back and thought, *I don't really want sex. I want to be loved and reassured.* But love and reassurance were all mixed up with sex in my mind along with anger, as if I couldn't feel one without the rest.

"Then I decided I would tell Peter I wanted to go home, but I sensed that if we goofed on this, we'd really be headed for trouble. Most of all, though, I was scared that he might get angry at me in front of all those people."

"What happened the next day?" I asked.

"Peter was the first one to speak in the group, and that terrified me," she said. "I thought it would be like that wife attacking her husband. He led off with my family, how they were always interfering. Then he started in on money. I just froze up. I didn't want to hear. There we were in a group of strangers and my husband was shouting at me!

"I couldn't move till one of the group, an older woman, came over and took my hands down from my head. There I was, covering my ears to block out Peter's anger! Later the leader asked me, 'Would you like to tell us how you and Peter usually work out your differences?'

"I just shook my head, and there was this awful silence till Peter said, 'We never work them out. When an argument gets out of hand we just hop into bed.' I think he was trying to be funny, but no one laughed, least of all me. Suddenly I had a glimpse of just what I had been doing, using sex not as an expression of love, but as a way to avoid our problems—and our anger.

"It isn't easy even now that we're aware of what we're doing," she went on. "The hardest thing is to really let go, to say what you truly feel. I try to use what I learned about listening from that weekend. No matter how angry Peter gets now, I listen. And you know, the more I learn to listen to him, the more he listens to me—and the easier it is to tell him just how I feel about things."

By expressing her feelings and standing firm when she knew she was right Wanda began to realize she could risk being angry. She didn't have to use sex to block it.

Now she and Peter both agree that they enjoy sex without fighting beforehand. "Oh, sometimes we kid around and pretend to argue, but it's all play." Sex, Wanda understands, should be an expression of closeness and love instead of a defense against anger or an escape from problems.

Expressing Anger Sexually

A young man brags to his friends, "Sure I knock my old lady around a little before we ball—she has to know who's boss." The odds are this man has learned to equate masculinity and sex with open aggression. Eventually his erection comes to depend on how much anger he can generate.

While this man expresses his anger in physical violence, another may use anger to prevent sexual performance. He may lose his erection as he is about to enter a woman, or he may ejaculate prematurely, and the act will be over before the woman has any pleasure. She has been effectively punished.

In depriving a woman of pleasure, a man is also punishing himself with impotence. Anger is the cause, but it is suppressed from his partner and himself. He just can't deal with his hostile feelings. They make him too vulnerable or too guilty.

He also fears being powerless and out of control. As a solution he opts for impotence. He may be punishing himself, but he also has a sexual weapon to punish his partner. Often such a man will say, "I don't understand why this only happens with you." Behind the lack of understanding is the pointing finger. He places the blame on his lover, hinting at her lack of femininity or sexual attractiveness. He may even feel sad about it all, covering up his underlying angry feelings. Even his small stab at hostility, "It only happens with you," is indirect.

There are some men who are so terrified of their inner anger that unconsciously they feel that having intercourse will cause them to literally explode inside the woman, blowing her apart. Often this rage is not directed at the woman the man is making love to. Instead it's a smouldering rage directed at all women.

Rage linked to sex isn't a masculine prerogative. Some women have sexual fantasies that are so terrifying to them they turn frigid rather than face them in sexual response. On one level, they want to hurt men and they see their vaginas as instruments to crush and mutilate men's penises. But on another level, they wish to protect men from their rage. Often such women bury their anger so successfully that they seem helpless and fragile.

Other angry women reject men by withholding sex. They plead illness or fatigue. It seems odd that helplessness, fragility, illness, or fatigue should all be direct results of anger—but anger finds strange outlets when we try to suppress it.

The ways we express anger sexually are many and varied for both men and women. Many young people have heightened the intensity of anger between the sexes. One aspect of today's sexual freedom is greater openness of fear and anger. Young men speak of women in terms of "ripping them apart" or "fucking up her mind." This open anger can cause some men to withdraw from women. Others become extremely passive and still others, unable to deal with their anger, become impotent.

Many women, angry themselves at this behavior, protect themselves by refusing to feel compassion, love, or desire. The combination of outward hostility and seething inner anger in both sexes leads these young people to the elimination of intimacy in their sexual encounters or relationships.

While men can express their anger physically, few women have the physical strength to overcome a man. They manage, however, to get their blows in indirectly. One woman, pregnant with her fourth child, confessed to her doctor, "I didn't want this baby, but I was so damned furious with him that night that I forgot to put in my diaphragm!"

A strange time to forget, it turned out. Her husband had just confessed to her that he had been sleeping with her best friend. On the surface she had understood and forgiven, but underneath she was seething. Her anger built until it reached the proportion of rage, and in the bedroom she got her peculiar sort of revenge.

In cases like this the bedroom becomes an arena of hate and anger. Lovers become combatants, but neither can win the fight.

Risking Anger

There is an old saying, *Never go to bed angry.* It should be amended to, *Never go to bed angry if you're going to wake up angry.* This doesn't mean that you should hold your anger in. To the contrary, never store it up!

First, learn to recognize when you are angry. Then, confront your lover with your annoyances, your irritations and aggravations *at the time it happens.* Don't bank your anger. The interest you'll draw isn't worth it.

What if your angry feelings always surface when you are in bed? Don't use sex to discharge them, and don't refuse sex as a way of getting your own back. Instead, try saying, I feel very angry at you. I feel that it isn't fair to either one of us to have sex now. Let's talk about how we both feel.

The *I feel* messages are less hostile, less threatening than an outright statement of *I am angry* or *I don't want sex.*

Don't expect your partner to fall right in with you, but if you stand firm and are secure within yourself and in your relationship, the message will get across. *I want to talk it out. You mean enough to me to try to work out what it is that makes me angry.*

Know the risks you are taking when you allow your anger to surface. If you feel that the chance of rejection is too great, go back in time and try to remember what you felt as a child when you expressed your anger. Are you still that child expecting rejection and loss of love?

Assess your anger, the degree of it. Ask yourself, do I feel less of a person when I'm angry?

Keep track of when and how your anger occurs, of what sets it off, how it's tied up with sex, and above all—look for a pattern.

The same method should apply to your lover's anger at you. Listen to it and try to determine how much of it is justified. Answer only the relevant part. Don't be pulled into unfair or unrelated bypaths.

If the anger always occurs before, during, or after sexual intercourse, try telling your lover, *I know that you're angry with me. I'm not sure why, but I'd like to talk it out. I can't make love if I feel you're hostile. Our being together in sex means too much to me.*

If the anger occurs right after sex or the next morning, you may have to confront your partner with what is happening and how you feel about it. Perhaps your lover is not aware of what he's doing.

If you care about another person and you want an intimate relationship, go slow—but stand firm. You have a right to know why anger is directed against you.

There are just as many risks in confronting another person's anger as there are in expressing your own. If you are frightened when anger occurs, use the same trip back into childhood to try to recall how you felt then when anger or hostility was directed against you. Tell your partner about these feelings. If he or she isn't interested in changing, if, by risking honesty, you will lose that relationship, then you must decide how important that relationship is.

A good, hard look at how you feel about yourself as a sexual person, and how much you want an intimate sexual relationship should be the key to how much risking you can handle.

A large part of sexual maturity is the assumption of responsibility for your own feelings and emotions. Anger is as much a part of an intimate sexual relationship as are love and caring. It is acceptable to be angry, to express your own anger and to receive another's. Recognize that fact and deal with it—and it will not sabotage or destroy the intimacy of sex.

Eight

Intimacy Begins With a Gentle Touch

First Experiences

We start experiencing intimacy even before birth. We first taste security in the warm darkness of our mother's womb, where, surrounded by comforting fluid, we float and rock gently to the reassurance of a steadily beating heart. It is our first experience with body intimacy, and never again will we be so close, in a physical sense, to another human being.

Leaving this cozy place, we struggle out into a world of noise, light, and violent sensations. There we are exposed to the brilliant glare of the delivery room, the loud voices, and the rude yanking that often make birth the first trauma of our lives.

We now know that the trauma can be lessened when the warmth of the womb is replaced by the embrace of the mother's arms. Some hospitals, recognizing this, place the new born baby on his mother's stomach even before the umbilical cord is cut. There, the warmth and touch of a mother's body can soothe the child.

Later, in this ideal situation, after the cord is cut and the baby bathed, the child is returned to its mother to hold in her arms. If the father is there, he too is allowed to hold his child. For parents, holding their newborn baby and feeling the touch of its tiny body, its soft skin and its gentle movement is a profoundly joyful experience. For the baby, secure in his mother's or father's arms, his head against a human breast, there is comfort in the familiar beat of a heart. As a parent touches, fondles, smiles, and coos at the child, the intimate bond is created, a rapport that answers one of the most basic of all human needs—touch.

Today most of us are aware of the need for touching babies, but many of us must still be reminded and reassured that it is all right to cuddle a baby, to comfort him when he cries, to hold him and to rock him.

Most parents can do this, but for some it is very difficult, and for others almost impossible. They love their children no less, but because they themselves had little experience with such touch and handling in their own childhood, they are unable to show it as parents. They handle their children in an impersonal, often rigid way.

But if the lack in the parents fosters a lack in the children, where do you break the chain? And can it be done? I became very aware of this question when I spent several weekends with young friends, one group in upstate New York, the other at New York's famous seashore at Fire Island. The week with the first group began with a party in the not-quite-finished house that my friends were building themselves. It was a casual home with handbuilt and hand-me-down furniture.

There were five married couples with their children at the party, several unmarried couples, and a few single men and women. All of them were warm and friendly, and they welcomed me easily and comfortably. As the evening progressed, I became more and more intrigued by the way the adults and children enjoyed each other's company.

Carolyn sat on the couch with her three-week-old baby in a sling against her breast. She carried on an animated conversation with her friends, but from time to time she paused to smile down at her baby and to caress it. Later the baby's father, Ken, came over, bent down, and whispered softly to the child.

In the kitchen another couple had put their ten-month-old boy on the table and while the mother fed him the father watched. Later this mother went back to join the party in the living room and the father sat enjoying a few moments alone with his son.

As I stood in the kitchen doorway watching, all around me people were talking and laughing, but the ten-month-old was quiet and happy just to sit there on the kitchen table. Occasionally he reached out to touch his father's hand, and when he did the father would lean over and kiss the top of his son's head.

I watched for a while, then I moved closer to see how the child would react to a stranger coming into this intimate circle. He regarded me gravely, and as I reached out to stroke the soft skin of his cheek, he smiled. He accepted me with poise and trust.

Wandering back into the living room, I noticed two young children, about three and five, playing on the floor near the wood-burning stove. Occasionally an adult would stoop down and speak to them, and they would smile and answer back.

As the evening wore on, I waited for what we used to call "gangrene setting in." That was how we referred to the unbearable time when children begin to whine and complain for attention. But "gangrene" never set in with these families. One mother nursed her baby, and one of the fathers took a tired child upstairs to sleep, but there was no pushing baby or child aside.

I was watching parents who enjoyed having their children with them, and children who reacted to their parents' friends with self-assurance. Children and adults were comfortable with each other—and intimately involved.

While mothers and fathers carried on conversations with friends, they still found time to glance at their children and from time to time touch them. What was curious to me was that other adults in the room did not resent having the children there. It was as if there was a community of family, a community of intimacy.

I couldn't help but contrast that evening with another weekend I spent with a party on Fire Island the same year. It was late summer and "gangrene set in" almost as soon as the party began. Two couples came with babies who were promptly relegated to another room. Before the rest of the adults had drinks in their hands, the couples were trying to shoo the children outside to play, and "get them out of our hair."

There was a lot of joking about how they could get rid of the kids and have some time to themselves, and in less than an hour the demand for attention by the younger children got out of hand and cast a pall over the entire evening.

Finally, desperately, someone suggested that the older children take the little ones to town and buy them some pizza and ice cream.

One little girl hung back. "Daddy, you promised to show me how to clam," she cried. "You promised."

Daddy was busy talking to a friend. "Later, Sweetie," he said absently, without looking at her or touching her.

It was the child's mother who finally walked her to the door. "Daddy's busy," she said kindly. "Go along with the others. Now come on, Sweetie, don't be a pain!"

But Sweetie was a pain, and it took a lot of coaxing to send her off. I had mixed feelings as I realized that the more the parents pushed the children away, the more demanding the children became until finally the parents fell back on bribery with food.

The party was not an isolated incident that weekend. By Sunday night, when most of the fathers headed back to the mainland, the kids had declared an "anything-to-get-attention war."

In turn, each parent brushed his children aside or tried to buy them off with movies, food, money—anything for a few moments of dearly needed peace!

Two Ways to Love

Later I asked myself why there was so much tension between the parents and children in one group and so little in the other. Where was the closeness and intimacy I had seen and felt with the parents upstate and their children coming from? Why was it missing in the group from Fire Island? Had one group grown up with intimacy or had they learned how to show it to their children by themselves?

I thought about the two groups and decided to return to both places to interview the parents. I prepared a few questions, but for the most part I just let the mothers and fathers talk.

I found that the one thing both groups had in common was a genuine love for their children. When I asked, "Do you feel you have an intimate relationship with your children," the answers differed slightly within each group, but a great deal between the two groups.

One of the parents from Fire Island said, "I want to be close to my boy, but what do you have to do to get close to a kid? Spend day and night with him?"

Another expressed it this way, "My God, those summers at the island cost a bundle. We spend all that money so the kids can be on the beach and have fun, and all they do is hang on to me. I love them, sure, but how intimate can you be with kids of three and seven?"

A third father declared, "I come out for a little rest after a hectic, miserable, hot week in the city and the kids are on my back! Sure I want to see them, but I have rights too. I'm just not a very intimate person. I need my privacy, and I need to relax with people my own age."

A father upstate had this to say about his children: "From the beginning he's been *our* child, not *her* child. We went through the birth together. Hell, I held my kid when he was only a few minutes old! That's as intimate as you can get."

His wife added, "My mother thought I was crazy to nurse the baby. She said, 'Get her on schedule and prop the bottle.' She wanted me to make it easy for myself, but she couldn't seem to understand the joy I got from holding my baby, touching her, feeling her at my breast."

Another mother remarked, "We're intimate people. We touch a lot and I get a great feeling from cuddling my kid and watching him grin up at me. You know, this intimacy thing works both ways."

Her husband joined in, "I don't feel that my child's cutting into my time. I look at the time I spend with her as my time too."

From the interviews it became clear to me that there were many forces at work in both groups and in each family. The upstate parents kept saying that they wanted to raise their children differently from the way they had been raised. They stressed closeness and were convinced that the father should be completely involved in the care of the child.

"I know my mother loved me," one woman told me. "But she never kissed or hugged me. I used to long for any kind of physical affection. I even used to pretend I was sick just to have her touch my forehead. How I missed it! I guess it was then, even as a child, that I decided that my baby would never miss any of the cuddling and kissing and closeness that I was denied.

"When my baby was born, I couldn't wait to hold her and touch her. In a way I think I was mothering myself by mothering her."

This makes very good sense. This young woman was willing to risk being close to her own baby, and she understood she needed very good reassuring support. "I'm lucky because my husband understands my need. He taught me to touch and be touched, not only in sex, but in our everyday life."

But she might have gone the other route. She could have learned the lesson of "nontouching" so well that as an adult she became cold and withdrawn. One of my Fire Island mothers had a similar childhood background, but she was unable to take the risk of intimacy with her baby.

"He's impossible!" she told me. "I want to love him, but he hates to be held."

After spending an afternoon with her it became evident that she was uncomfortable touching and handling her baby. While we talked she put the child on the couch next to her and held his bottle with one hand. The only time she touched him was to wipe off his chin. Finally, when he was finished, she picked him up, burped him, and took him into the bedroom to change his diaper. Her movements were efficient, but mechanical, with little touching or warmth.

The baby, in turn, reacted by nervously squirming and pulling away as the woman became more and more upset. "He just hates to be held," she explained again defensively.

Here was a mother who loved her baby and took scrupulous care of him. She fed her baby and kept him warm and clean, and as a responsible mother she assumed she had taken care of all his needs. In discussing her own parents, she mentioned wistfully, "We were never a very demonstrative family. We were never very close."

How did these two women define closeness? "It isn't enough," said one upstate father thoughtfully, "to be emotionally close. You have to be physically close too. I didn't have much of that from my parents, and I guess in a way I'm making up for it with my kid by spending time with him. I happen to think that's more valuable than anything I could buy."

The Fire Island group talked of time too, but most of the parents, particularly the fathers, felt that they were too pressured and worked too hard to be able to give their children "that much time." They also felt that the social and material advantages they offered their children made up for that lack. This group of parents asked questions of me—and of themselves—that the other group never touched on. Were they being too permissive? Was it wrong for a child to have his own television or telephone? Is my child an underachiever? This last question came from the mother of a six-year-old!

These parents were much more uneasy about their children than the upstate group, but later, going over my notes, I found that the two groups shared a common background. They were all children of comfortable, middle-class parents and most of them had been raised in or around the city. All of them were well-educated, articulate men and women. But while the Fire Island group was set on the path of upward mobility for themselves and their children, the parents upstate had consciously rejected that way. And it was this latter group that seemed better able to be intimate with their children.

It does not follow that to have an intimate relationship with your children you must renounce upward mobility, take to the country, and build your own house. Nor does it follow that fathers must find jobs that keep them close to home, or that mothers must nurse their babies for them to grow up into adults capable of intimacy.

What is evident is that intimacy is a learned behavior. From the moment of birth, a baby is like a little sponge soaking up patterns of how to behave. A child is born with the ability to learn to speak, but first he must hear and imitate the human voice. Like speech, the ability to be intimate is within all of us. What is needed to trigger it off is the experience of intimacy.

This *experience of intimacy* is what the upstate parents were striving to give their children. They touched and held them, took the time to speak to them in a reassuring way and to smile and laugh with them. They seldom pushed their children away. To the contrary, they tried to gather them close, not only in a physical way, but in a deeper way that said, without words, *You are a part of me. I am a part of you. We are a family.*

Children, reassured, don't demand an excess of attention or constant physical closeness. They know attention and closeness are available if they need it. A mutual acceptance and interdependence exists between parents and children.

The Fire Island parents, on the other hand, kept trying to make time for themselves. They felt they were entitled to it and couldn't understand why their children didn't see it too. To get their privacy, they pushed their children away. As one mother said, half-joking, "I can't wait to get them all into school and out of my hair. Kids can get to be a drag."

What seemed to happen to these children, even to the babies, was an inability to get enough of the physical closeness that they needed. Indeed, they often *were* a "drag" as they whined and clung to their parents. The more the parents tried to get free of them, the more the children demanded attention.

One group felt that caring for their children was a task, while the other believed it was a pleasure to be shared by both parent and child.

The upstate families seem to me close to one end of a broad spectrum of intimacy while the Fire Island children lie somewhere in the middle. At the far end of the spectrum are those children completely deprived of love and hope. None of the Fire Island children were that bad. What they lacked was closeness with their parents, the reassurance by word and touch that they were part of an intimate, caring family.

We can project that many of these children who were denied this closeness in childhood will be reluctant to risk it as adults. Some of them may not even know what they are lacking. They will assume, as their parents did, that acquiring a wife, a husband, or children is synonymous with intimacy, that the outward trappings of a family are substitutes for closeness, love, and care.

It is these men and women who have a tough time waking from the dream of happy marriage to the reality of a life with intimacy, with sharing and caring.

In the next chapter we will discover how intimacy can be cultivated, even in families which have trouble with it.

Nine

Overcoming a Hazardous Family Inheritance

The Hazardous Family

The family is many things to many people. For some of us it is a comfortable enclave where we learn love, trust, and caring, a protected place where we can take our earliest risks with intimacy, knowing that we will not be hurt or rejected.

But for others the family is a hazard and a barrier to intimacy. All parents transmit their own behavior to their children, and if that behavior is cold or closed or destructive, the child will be afraid to take those first risks. When those old vulnerabilities interfere with the way we act and react with others, then we must begin to search for solutions in our pasts. Can we drop that excess baggage? Can we reshape our backgrounds, reinterpret our childhood?

Is it possible to overcome the backgrounds that produce intimacy-defeating situations?

It is possible to do so. By understanding our past we can change and strengthen ourselves enough to take a chance with those closest to us. How do we get to understand those old patterns of behavior? We must ask ourselves some hard questions and examine what we do today in the light of those old vulnerabilities. Try these questions, and try answering them honestly and thoughtfully.

—Are you treating your husband, wife, or lover as a father or mother? Are you trying to find, in them, the things your own parents denied you?

—Do you compete with your husband, wife, or lover as you once did with your brother or sister? Does the competition satisfy your needs?

—When you have problems with your children, do you discipline them as you were once disciplined? Is it because you believe in discipline, or in spite of the fact that you feel discipline is wrong?

—Do you see your fellow workers in terms of your original family? Are you jealous of them as you were of your brother or sister? Do you constantly seek approval from the people above you as you did from your mother and father?

—Does any of this apply to friends? Do you carry the old family relationships into friendships?

—Are you really intimate with your children, your husband, wife, lover—or do you think of yourself as a nonintimate person? If so, are you reliving your role in your original family?

—Were you labeled as a child? Are you living that label? Do you label your children, wife, lover, friends?

In answering these questions, look for repeated patterns of behavior, patterns that seem to be preventing the kind of intimate relationships you would like to have with the important people in your life.

Be sensitive to your own emotions. Instead of telling yourself, "I feel anxious, guilty, depressed, stupid, or unhappy," ask yourself, "Why do I feel this way? What is happening right now to trigger off these negative feelings? Am I this way because of a real reason, or does this situation remind me of something that happened when I was a child?"

Most feelings of anxiety, guilt, and depression have their origins in your family background, or if they originate in today's situations they are strengthened and blown up out of proportion by a childhood experience. What was there in your own family that made you feel this way? Try to dig it out of your past. Were you unable to be what your parents wanted? Do you come from a family that couldn't communicate? Were you labeled as a child? Did you feel unloved, unwanted in your own family?

Once you begin to understand that today's pattern of behavior can be closely tied to childhood, you can begin to risk cutting those ties. Remember, you are no longer that defenseless child in your original family, vulnerable and in need of protection. You are an adult now, with adult abilities and strengths. You also have the ability to understand your past and the strength to risk changing your future.

To see how one family almost changed their patterns of behavior, let me introduce the Smiths, mother, father, daughter, and son. Each moved in a different emotional space, and seldom did one make intimate contact with the other. The Smiths had very little experience in family closeness. They cared about their children, but they were unable to take a chance and show that caring.

Father Smith had assumed his own father's role, the strict disciplinarian. He was rigid in his thinking and in his attitude toward his wife and children. There was even a sense of measured deliberation in the way he talked and moved. Outside the family he was known as a man who was set in his ways, unbending.

When his son or daughter did something well, Father Smith didn't know how to show approval. He seldom touched his children or his wife affectionately, but still, as the mother told her son and daughter, "Daddy is a good provider. He really cares about us!"

His wife was replaying the emotions of her own childhood, a childhood that was torn apart when her mother deserted the family. In her own way Mother Smith had shut out her children and husband. She was a part of their lives, making the meals, doing the laundry, keeping up the house—but all too often she was emotionally absent, locked into the feelings of that frightened little girl of her childhood.

The Smiths seldom called each other by name. Instead they sent indirect messages.

MOTHER: (To her husband) Your son is acting up again. (To her son) I told you I'd tell your father when he got home.

FATHER: She tells me the school called up.

MOTHER: Tell your father what you did.

SON: Nothing!

FATHER: Nothing? The school wouldn't call her about nothing.

MOTHER: I just can't handle him.

FATHER: If the school called, he's in the wrong. He's too big to whip but not too big to punish. No more Saturday afternoons off. He'll stay home and clean up the yard.

What happened here was typical of the Smiths. Three people in a family are talking *about* each other and *at* each other, but not *to* each other. They refer to each other as she, him, your son, your father, as if subconsciously aware that not using a person's name is a strong device for avoiding intimacy. It also denies kinship. If he is *your* son, how can he be my responsibility?

The Smiths' son was sixteen and although he acted up in school, he was already as rigid as his father. He had few friends because he demanded too much. Things had to be done his way. He was suspicious of everyone and afraid to risk new relationships. He spent hours alone in his room listening to records, using privacy as a defense. Resentful of his father and guilty about his mother, he still longed for a closer relationship with both.

His sister was fourteen, and she moved in her own world too. On the surface she seemed much warmer and happier than her brother, but it was just a mask to hide a desperate need for intimate contact. She remembered that as a little child her father would hold her in his lap, and she still treasured the memory of that protective tenderness. There was so little of it.

As a teenager she tried to recapture it with older boys and at fourteen she began to be sexually promiscuous. At home there seemed no way of getting the physical or emotional touch she needed, so like her brother she withdrew into her room and saw the rest of the family only at meals.

The Smiths, as a family, were well on their way to that isolated life that could make the son see intimacy as a risk too terrible to take while the daughter saw it as a treasure so great that she would go to any lengths to get it. Fortunately, the Smiths were survivors, and when their son was involved in a serious car accident, something happened to the family that caused all of them to change.

Driving the family car, the son was hit broadside by another car running a red light. The frightened parents and daughter rushed to the hospital, only to be told that the boy was in surgery and would be there for several more hours.

Stunned, frightened, and anxious, the three of them sat in the waiting room on a couch, the father rigid and apart as always, the mother withdrawn into a corner of the couch, her face a mask. It was the daughter who broke down and began to cry. "Oh God, will he be all right, Daddy? Will he be all right?"

The father's tight control melted in that moment, and he put his arms around her. The sound of her voice saying "Daddy" released years of buried emotions. Here was his daughter turning to him for comfort and somewhere in the hospital his other child lay injured, maybe dying! Together, tears in their eyes, the father and daughter reached for each other and embraced.

The mother, watching them, still sat frozen in her corner until the two, realizing her pain and torn by their own anguish, went to her. For the first time in years the three touched and held each other. The mother stroked her daughter's hair and held tight to her husband's hand. The daughter touched her mother's face and in that moment of great trauma the three of them risked a deep physical intimacy—and were rewarded for that risk.

Often a serious and terrible trauma, an accident, a death, a misfortune can serve as a catalyst to break through some of the barriers that separate the people within a family—provided that behind the barriers there is still love and caring. But all too often, in families with little intimacy a trauma can tear apart an already fragile relationship.

The Smiths changed for the better, but the change lasted only as long as their boy was in danger. Mr. Smith's genuine concern for his son allowed him to move out of the role of disciplinarian, to express some of his real feelings of love and caring. While the boy was on the critical list, the family risked a deeper, more intimate relationship. The parents spoke to each other and to their children, not as strangers, but as friends.

They comforted one another and the mother began to touch and kiss her son. When they left the hospital, the parents and daughter turned to each other for reassurance and affection.

Unhappily, the newfound intimacy didn't last,

perhaps because it hadn't come to them through true understanding. The accident had brought them together, and afterward the father returned to some of his old rigidity and the mother began to retreat into herself. Both of the parents had been locked into their isolated behavior for too long. They were still afraid of their own feelings, and still had a long way to go. They will probably always have some difficulty with intimacy, but there has been a change. There is the beginning of trust and caring in the children. Both are learning to be intimate—late, perhaps, but better late than not at all.

Perhaps they have learned enough from this to risk a genuine intimacy outside the family, and, most important of all, not perpetuate the same inability when they marry and have children.

The Counterfeit Emotion

There often seems to be a nongenetic inheritance of intimacy within a family. A child learns to be intimate, or to fear intimacy, early in life, and, as we have seen, he learns it from his parents. In turn, he passes on this learning to his own children. Sometimes, unable to risk it, the individual settles for a pseudointimacy, a counterfeit of the real thing. Clair and Roger were like that.

People had always thought of their family as close and successful. "Happy overachievers," Roger once called them jokingly. His son, John, was in his third year at medical school, and his daughter, Kathy, was starting her first year at Brown. Clair always maintained that the secret of a loving family is children who trust their parents enough to tell them anything.

But the loving, closeknit family was only a facade. Kathy had been seeing a therapist without any of their friends knowing about it. It was something her mother had suggested and Kathy, recognizing her own need, had agreed.

On her last visit, before school began, the therapist said, "I guess you're all excited about going off to college."

Kathy, tense and nervous, burst into tears. "I decided not to go. I want to stay home," she said miserably.

"But you told me you were accepted at Brown."

"Well, I just won't go. I'm too . . . too scared!"

After a flood of tears and several handfuls of Kleenex, the whole story came out. Kathy had been an "A" student all through high school, but that wasn't what her parents really wanted. "Oh, they liked the idea of a daughter with straight As, but I knew that what really pleased them was my popularity. I was elected Homecoming Queen, and that was their idea of achievement. I was the fair-haired lady that day."

When Kathy was accepted at Brown, the only one in her school, all her mother talked about was the clothes she would need and all the fun she'd have, the boys she'd have to choose from. The more she talked, the worse Kathy felt. In the end she simply refused to go to college.

"I don't want to go anywhere or see anyone. To tell you the truth, I just don't know where I'm at."

"Have you talked this over with your mother?" the therapist asked.

"Everyone's taken in by my mother," Kathy said bitterly. "She talks up a storm—sometimes I feel as if I'm drowning in her words. She's always insisting we're such a close family. 'My children confide in me.' Well, I figured out a long time ago that as long as I tell her what she wants to hear she'll listen."

"And your father?"

"He's just as bad. He still sees me as his popular

little girl. All I could think of when I was accepted at college was, suppose I go and I'm not popular?"

The therapist shook her head. "I see what you mean, but it's usually hard to talk to parents. But I have an idea," she suggested. "Why don't you try a tape recording? Put down just what you feel when you're not so emotionally charged, and let them listen to it when they're alone."

"Do you think it would work?"

"They love you, and that's half the battle."

Uncertain, but willing to try anything to get closer to her parents, Kathy recorded all the things she felt. Her mother, when she heard about it, immediately protested. "In our family we don't need tape recorders. We can still talk to each other."

Kathy sighed. "Perhaps you can, but I can't. Please! Will you and Dad listen to the tape? I'm going out for a while."

When she came home later she found that not only had they listened, but they had each taped replies. Within a week they were communicating honestly and intimately—on tape. Kathy had broken through the first barrier, had forced them to listen and in turn had heard their side of the problem.

By using a tape recorder Kathy and her parents were effectively distancing themselves from the problem and they were able to deal with it on a rational level. As Kathy told her therapist later, "I was able to let out a lot more on tape—and I couldn't avoid hearing them out. I found emotions are scary, especially if you bottle them up, but no matter what you say into the tape, the other person has to listen. I mean, if you're not there how can they be defensive? Now I feel so much closer to them both."

For Clair, the tapes brought home the realization that she had tried to live vicariously through her daughter. She began to see Kathy as a person in her own right with her own goals. It was painful for her to admit that her daughter wasn't the "happy, secure girl" she bragged about to her friends, but she understood her own need to brag. As long as she could convince herself that her children were achievers she could calm her own inner anxiety and guilt. She could tell herself she was a good mother. The proof: her family.

Kathy's father found it hard to sort out his own emotions about his "pretty little girl." He couldn't relate to her as a woman, couldn't find the intimacy he wanted in part because he was bewildered by her obviously superior intellect.

The transition from tape to face-to-face discussions, and all the intimacy it brought, came slowly and wasn't easy. Old habits of defensiveness, of pretense and lack of trust died reluctantly.

"I kept thinking I mustn't disappoint them," Kathy told her therapist. "They might not love me if I didn't conform, and how can you be intimate with anyone when you have those blocks?"

"Well, you took a risk by confronting them," her therapist said. "Was it worth it?"

"Oh God, yes! I'm so much closer to them now, especially my mother, and that's funny because for the first time I feel as if I'm really a separate person. I don't know the new me too well yet, but I told Mom that part of growing up is finding out who you are. Once I know that I can find out what I want to do about school and my life." She grinned. "Do you know what Mom said to me? She said, 'I'm twice your age and I'm just beginning to know myself.' "

Labeling the Children

Genuine affection between parents should be there before children are born. Caring, tenderness, trust, and unselfish love between a husband and wife are more than a learning experience for a child. These things are his inheritance. They allow him the courage to take his own first risks with intimacy—within his family.

When parents battle out their ambivalence in the family arena, they are at least more evenly matched than a parent battling against his own child—and many parents do battle their children. Their weapons are more subtle, but no less deadly. Teasing, labeling, rejection, and withdrawal can destroy any child's attempts at intimacy.

But children aren't the only victims. One parent can attack another. Consider the family where a dialogue like this can take place.

FATHER: My God, can't you even balance a checkbook?

MOTHER: I'll admit you're better at figures than I am. (After a pause) Joe's wife tells me he got a big raise. It's a shame you're not more aggressive at the job.

A good many areas of sarcasm and hostility are covered here. In another family the hostility is even more obvious.

FATHER: What have you been doing all day? Coffee klatching with your friends? Is that why you forgot to call about the car?

MOTHER: You told me you'd stop by and pick it up on the way home, but I suppose you forget a lot of things when you go out with the boys for a drink.

FATHER: What is that supposed to mean?

MOTHER: Nothing. Dinner's ready. I had to warm it up again for you.

What does a son learn from hearing this or similar conversations between his parents week after week and year after year? Women are not to be trusted. They are undependable. Men are the dominant ones and they must keep women in line.

A daughter gets still another message. She becomes aware that women must be subtle in their defense and attack. Sarcasm and veiled criticism are effective weapons in any battle between the sexes. No matter who wins the battle, the children lose, for they grow up with a distorted idea of intimacy between husband and wife. A husband teasing his wife, or a wife digging at her husband are sending messages to their children. Beware of getting close to another person or you'll end up like this.

But on the positive side, children also notice when one parent does something unselfish for another. They are aware if their parents trust each other and really care for each other. They suck up all the positive and negative feelings and emotions generated between the two most important people in their lives.

It is amazing to me how many young people have told me, "My parents never kiss each other," or "They're always kissing and hugging their friends, but never each other."

It is often painful to examine one's own childhood and see how intimacy was destroyed. In my own family, my sister Betty was an example of labeling. Now, years later, I can realize that Betty was always out of synch with the rest of the family. She talked and moved too fast, cried too easily, and even laughed too quickly.

My father teased her constantly. "She hasn't the brains God gave a chicken," was his favorite expression, said with a disarming smile, but still said. Dad teased us all, but he was unusually hard on Betty. Mother's defense didn't help. "Betty's not really stupid. She just never stops to think."

As a child, Betty begged for attention, any kind of attention, and Mother would say, "Betty keeps at you so. She wants to be loved—but she's so hard to love."

When she was only six Betty was already typecast as "not too smart and not too lovable." By the time she was an adult, she thought of herself as "stupid and dopey." She married right after high school—what else could a "stupid" girl do? And she spent most of her life trying to make up for being unloved.

Perhaps I am too harsh with my parents. When Betty needed money they always helped. When she was ill they were concerned, and they were always in touch. But they could never give her the kind of love and approval she needed as a child. Perhaps the fault was that they were labelers. They saw all their children in terms of, *The stupid one, The smart one, The cold one, The mixed-up one.*

Betty might have been different as an adult if she had been able to understand and recreate the experiences of her childhood. In identifying her feelings as a child with those as an adult, she could have dealt with them not as a vulnerable little girl, but as a grown woman. As it was, she went through life longing for intimacy, but always sabotaging her intimate relationships. She was driven to prove that childhood label, *stupid Betty,* over and over again.

Old Vulnerabilities Die Hard

An accident brought the Smith family out of their shells. A family locked into such rigid behavior for so long cannot risk complete change, but any breakthrough, no matter how small, helps. Intimacy is not an all-or-nothing proposition.

Kathy took a step forward when she recognized that she had a problem with her parents. She took a giant step forward when she broke the communication barrier. Many of us are not as closely tied to our original families as Kathy was. We have grown up and moved away physically, but we left home carrying the excess baggage of old vulnerabilities.

You must remember that when you look back at your original family the lens you use is often distorted by what you want to see and what you are afraid to see. We tend to see our family as all good or all bad, seeing only black and white and none of the gray in between.

We can't completely cut ourselves off from that original family. We all have a strong need for family ties. Many of us are exposed to a philosophy that tells us to do our own thing, be our own self, and we often misinterpret this to mean, "Do what you want and damn the consequences to friends, lovers, or family."

As adults we are capable of understanding, forgiving, and loving parents who may have hurt or disappointed us in the past. We can do it if we look for shared experiences that created warm moments of love and closeness. Usually we do not have to give up our own values or independence in order to heal old wounds. We can reach out and touch those people who are still a part of us just as we will always be a part of them.

The *self* cannot exist selfishly and alone. Self must be a part of the world, a part of the immediate environment, a part of a friendship network.

In the next chapter we will discuss ways to get in touch with friendship, to strengthen it, to respect it. We'll learn that intimacy with others is not possible without self-intimacy. We have learned to love and accept ourselves, and now we will see how we can love and accept others.

Ten

Intimacy Among Friends

Boys and Girls Together

In a song from the musical comedy, *Pal Joey*, the world discovers "how to make true lovers out of friends." It is, I believe, far more difficult to make true friends out of lovers—or, to take it a step farther, to make intimate friends out of men and women whether they are lovers or not, and especially when they are *not* lovers. But it can be done, and it's easier now when young people are not trapped into sexual stereotypes.

Such an intimate friendship can change the course of a person's life. Take Nancy and Tim for instance. They lived next door to each other, and they were friends since they were ten years old. Nancy remembered the day when none of her girlfriends were around, and she saw Tim shooting baskets in his backyard.

She knew him, but they had never played together. Now she came over and watched him for a while, then asked, "Can I try it?"

Tim tossed her the ball, and after three tries she made a basket. "Not bad!" he commented, taking the ball and demonstrating. "Look, what you gotta do is stand like this and line it up. See?" He dropped the ball in. "Want to try again?"

"Sure," Nancy replied. That afternoon both children had a good time playing and just being together. During the rest of the summer, Nancy picked up a few pointers from Tim on basketball, and one rainy afternoon she invited him over to make brownies. What started as a simple childhood encounter grew throughout their adolescence and afterward into a deep and lasting friendship. Tim could risk being friendly to Nancy that first day because no other boys were around to tease him about playing with a girl. Both children were open and accepting of each other. They weren't locked into the stereotypes of *girl's play* and *boy's play*, and so they could be friends. Their relationship to each other was something special because they shared past experiences as well as present ones.

When Nancy had a devastating love affair in high school it was Tim's shoulder she cried on, and he turned to her for understanding and compassion when his brother was reported missing in Vietnam. Throughout the years of growing up they managed to sustain their close feelings for each other. They are not lovers. They do not see each other as a brother and sister. Instead, they are friends—intimate, loving friends.

Nancy and Tim remained friends, even though they each belonged to separate groups, a fact which made them different from a lot of young people. As children grow older, groups can become a source of intimacy. Early in adolescence boys "bond" together not only in team sports, but in social activities. They "hang out" and "horse around" in front of the local candy store or bowling alley, or they "cruise" the streets of small towns, *American Graffiti* style. As a group, they spend long hours in discussing girls, drinking, and sex.

Tim and his friends got a sense of belonging out of the group, and in this way the bonding has a positive aspect. It taught the boys cooperation, fair play, and some degree of unselfishness—as well as training them in the group myths. A young man learns that his identity and self-esteem is tied to the group. But bonding often insists on a code of rigid masculine behavior that follows old cultural rules and roles.

To be accepted by the group, to be part of the "male" community, each member must conform. In turn the group supports him. Often, if a boy cannot live up to the group's expectations, the group will find a way out for him. "Howie can't catch worth a damn, but he knows all the rules."

Group acceptance is based on the group definition of masculinity—and so is friendship. Unfortunately this sometimes leaves little room for individuality, and there is often an underlying uneasiness, a fear of not being like "the rest of the guys." Boys in groups settle for intimate friendship within the group, but they settle for the conformity of the group, rather than becoming complete individuals. How can you discover yourself if you are forced into role playing? And adolescence, traditionally, is a time of self-discovery.

If your interests become different from the group interests, if you become intrigued with books, or studies, or the arts while the group is into sports and sex, they might reject you. You're the "oddball." On the other hand, it is possible that the group might accept you and be a little proud of you, supporting your "oddness" as something to admire.

Often the bonding of adolescence carries over into adult life, and grown men try to recreate that old feeling of belonging. They equate the group with the best intimacy they've known. They're comfortable only in the company of other men, and happiest in a group. They love to retell the stories of high school sports, fraternity beer parties, Army adventures. The stories are often told to new groups, but the experiences are interchangeable. The new group understands, for the stories answer a need.

Unlike boys, adolescent girls are usually wary of bonding. Some may form cliques, not to reaffirm their femininity or reinforce friendship, but to exclude other girls. Young girls tend to measure their innate value in terms of popularity and their ability to attract boys.

While the boys compete on the football field, girls become involved in a much deadlier sport, a sport without team cooperation or fair play—the competition for boys' attention and for popularity. Each girl sees all other girls as opponents and each opponent as an enemy.

The adolescent girl is usually a mass of conflicts. In spite of the competition, she longs for friendship with another girl. To have a best friend is to be of value to another. A friend is someone to confide in, to share the often painful secrets of growing up—but the name of the feminine game is competition, and confiding has no place in the game. It makes betrayal more of a certainty than a risk.

While many girls fall into the trap of competitiveness, there are still others who form deep and lasting friendships. Ruth and Doloris are now in their thirties, and though they live in different parts of the country they still correspond regularly. Only last Christmas Doloris and her husband came east to visit Ruth and her family.

They first met in high school when Doloris, a shy and gentle girl, was transferred into Ruth's class. She was not accepted by most of the high school cliques, but Ruth, who shared a poetry class with her, admired the way she wrote and asked her advice about her own poetry. The two quickly found something in each other to admire, and Ruth risked offending the established cliques by befriending Doloris. It was worth the risk. She not only made a valuable new friend, but in spite of some snubs managed to keep her old ones.

Ruth got Doloris to join the drama club and Doloris, an avid reader, introduced Ruth to the Jalna series. They exchanged books, went to the library together, and were both in the class play.

"We always had something to talk about," Ruth said. "It wasn't just the books. It was tennis one year, then the debating team and of course boys. That was the real test of friendship, the year we both had crushes on the same guy.

"I was heartbroken when he asked Doloris out and I told her so. I had to tell someone, and I couldn't trust any of my other girlfriends with my secret. I knew I could trust Doloris. We understood each other and we cared about each other. We still do."

Between the Sexes

There are some people who manage to make and keep deep personal friendships with the other sex, but many of us are uneasy in such situations, acting as if men and women were members of different species. We pretend closeness, but retreat into the safety of roles. We doubt that close friendships are possible between men and women without sex rearing its head.

Melissa and Rod were able to make it as friends, but first they had to drop their role playing. "I almost blew it the first time I met Rod at a party," Melissa told me. "I liked the things he said. I thought he'd be a nice friend to have, but only a friend. I wasn't turned on sexually. But still I went through the whole ritual of *coming on* to him, all the silly flirting and meaningless teasing.

"When he didn't respond in the accepted masculine way it upset me and confused me. I felt uptight, insecure, and anxious, as if there must be something wrong with me. But I really did want to talk to him. He was a warm, interesting guy and we had lots of mutual interests. We had both studied Russian, and Rod was as much of a ballet freak as I was."

"Intellectually the vibes were right between Melissa and me," Rod confided. "But I didn't want to get involved in game playing and spoil the chance of a nice friendship."

"Now Rod and I have something unusual," Melissa declares. "We really are very close and I know that I can go to him if I have a problem just as he can come to me. We depend on each other and we really care about each other. I can trust him and turn to him in a pinch. I can't say that about a lot of people." Thoughtfully, she added, "I suppose we love each other in a nonsexual way."

How did it all come about? How did they manage to drop the role playing? It was Rod who managed to cut through the man-woman playacting. "I decided I'd take a chance. The worst she could do was tell me to 'Bug off!' I said, 'Look. I like you, and I like the way you think, but I'm just not ready for any sexual involvement with you. Can we really just be friends?"

"I was upset," Melissa confessed, "even though this was what I wanted. I felt rejected. I was all ready to snap out something sarcastic, when I thought, 'Hey! This is cool. Maybe we can be friends.' I put out my hand and said, 'Shake on it, partner!' and we both laughed and that was the start."

In our culture deep affection and love are acceptable within a family, a marriage, or between lovers. But when there is affection and love between a man and a woman who are just friends, it is not as acceptable. We're suspicious of close friends. If they're not having a little sexual thing going then one of them must be gay.

Americans find it hard to separate what they are from what they are supposed to be, the roles they think they should play. They equate sex with intimacy. When a man meets a woman, flirtation becomes a way of not relating, a counterfeit intimacy, and avoidance of true friendship.

There are times, of course, when flirtation is perfectly acceptable and fine. It's a grand way of relating to the other sex. But when it's your *only* way of relating to the other sex, then it closes off all chances for an intimate friendship.

If you are going to have an intimate relationship with someone of the other sex, decide first what kind of a relationship you want. If it's friendship, be frank about it from the beginning. Forget the flirting and risk, as Rod did, saying, "Let's be friends." Put it on a positive note. "I like the way you think —talk—your sense of humor—your politics—we've got a lot in common and I honestly don't want to spoil it. Let's be good friends."

Sometimes it won't work, especially if the other person is heavily into roles, or feels threatened if he or she is not allowed to function as a lover. However, sometimes it will work and the friendship that results will be worth it.

For many of us there is a safety in hiding behind the masks of flirtation, charm, submission, and aggression. We fear that if we become too intimate, too trusting, and too involved we will be betrayed. We realize that there is always the possibility, in an intimate friendship, that one friend will fall in love with the other. When this happens and the feeling is not reciprocated, the friendship usually suffers and eventually ends.

For those involved, there are loss, rejection, and hurt, and a sense of betrayal. In intimate friendship, as in any close relationship, there is always the risk that someone will get hurt. Rather than take the risk, many of us pretend to an intimacy that doesn't exist. We set up defenses and barricades to avoid involvement, to guard against anyone's getting too close.

The Pseudointimatizers

Sometimes the barricades we erect are so clever that we are completely unaware that they block intimacy. It took me a long time to realize that a couple I had known for years had many friends but were close to no one. They were frantic people who constantly surrounded themselves with crowds. A dinner party must have at least twenty people, and a night at the theater must be shared with at least four other couples. They had always managed to avoid intimacy, yet gave the illusion of having many "close, dear friends." They pretended interest by asking intimate questions, but they never listened to the answers. They acquired friends quickly but discarded them just as fast.

When a close friend of theirs, Selma, lost her husband, they found themselves unable to deal with the part of friendship that requires sharing another's grief. They were not deliberately cruel—they were just not able to become involved. They could have overcome the problem if they had been aware of the fact that they used people to block intimacy. But they would have had to take a risk.

When the husband of this couple complained to me that they wished they could help Selma, I suggested that they ask her up to their summer house for a week alone with them. But they couldn't risk that. They were willing to share a funny story, a good gossip, anything that was fun, but they were incapable of sharing anything sorrowful such as Selma's grief.

But sharing trouble can be a long step toward intimacy. During a severe blizzard last winter, three families who lived near one another were snowbound together in a rural farmhouse near Watertown, New York. I was fascinated by their story because of the contrast to my friends. Six adults and seventeen children lived in one small house for ten days. To conserve heat, the living room was converted into a dormitory. Isolated from the outside world, the three families lived communally under crowded conditions. They shared all the work, rationed their food, and kept themselves amused with conversation, cards, reading, television, charades, and endless storytelling.

They survived the ten days with only some minor irritations. In talking about it afterward, one woman said, "We have gotten to know our friends intimately, and the loneliness and despair of being stranded hasn't bothered us as much as it might have."

In those ten days, ordinary neighbors became such intimate friends that when the blizzard let up and one of the families prepared to leave, the others begged them to stay longer.

What made it possible for these families to become so intimate in ten days while the couple I knew for fifteen years were still strangers to me and their friends?

Intimacy, we have learned throughout this book, includes sharing, mutual trust, and caring. My friends never learned to share anything more than a good time. There was no mutual trust between them and me, and they didn't care about their friends any more than their friends cared about them. They had woven a web of superficial relationships.

The three families isolated by the snowstorm were forced by circumstances into sharing. They couldn't have survived without it. Trust was necessary in such a situation, and caring came inevitably. They were forced into intimacy—and liked what they experienced.

Liquor and Intimacy Don't Mix

In our modern world we recognize the need for trust and sharing, but we can't rely on a cataclysm to bring us together. To escape from the web of superficialities we turn to artificial intimatizers, one of the important ones being alcohol.

People who depend on liquor to break the intimacy barrier are rarely without a drink at a social gathering, and they feel threatened if their friends aren't drinking. They recognize liquor as the great intimatizer:

—Two martinis and I can talk to anyone.

—A drink makes me less shy.

—Let's have a booze, then we can do business.

—It's a way of breaking the ice, of really getting to know someone.

All of us have, at times, felt awkward, vulnerable, even scared in a social group, and most of us have used a drink to help us through. But when you find that the only way you can relate to people is with liquor, when you realize that once the drink wears off you are going to feel isolated and friendless, then liquor becomes a crutch and you should take a good look at what is happening to you. It seems sad that in our society so many people cannot reach out to an old friend, or make a new one without a couple of drinks under the belt.

Drinking is an accepted social ritual, and it has its good points as well as its bad in terms of intimacy. Most of us enjoy the camaraderie of a drink with our friends, just as we enjoy dinner with them. A drink lessens our tension and helps us unwind. For others it acts as a *fail safe.*

Take Judy. She can always be counted on to drink too much at a party. The next day she's on the phone to everyone trying to explain away her behavior. "I don't know what I said last night. I was bombed out of my mind. I'm sorry if I offended you, but I guess I just can't take martinis."

What Judy really can't take is rejection. She's afraid that if she reveals any part of herself she'll be slapped down. Her offer of friendship will become an embarrassment, a hurt, a rejection. Her inner loneliness, her sense of isolation becomes so desperate that she searches for an escape hatch, and finds it in liquor.

After a few drinks she begins to talk, to confide in others, to reveal a little bit of herself. For a few moments she breaks through her isolation and makes human contact. But the fear of rejection is still there, and so she keeps her perfect excuse. "I was bombed out of my mind!" In other words, "I wasn't responsible. No one can fault me or reject me." Judy has made a little foray into intimacy, has asked for friendship, but has kept her *fail safe*. Too much to drink.

Alcohol is Judy's intimatizer. Others may use marijuana. They claim it breaks down the barriers that separate them from their friends.

Unfortunately, most of these intimatizers turn us inward. We may get in touch with ourselves, but rarely with each other. The group passes a joint around and the act of sharing the joint gives the illusion that they are also sharing the experience. One friend may ask another how he feels, but there is very little intimate exchange. Instead there is emotional removal. Later, when the dope wears off, the isolation, the loneliness, the emptiness returns.

We can, however, overcome the fear of rejection without using pseudointimatizers. The way to do it is to try taking your risks in small steps. The next time you go to a party, before you have a drink or a joint:

—Speak to three people you know, even if it's just to ask how they are and what they're doing.

—Introduce yourself to three strangers.

—Strike up a conversation with a stranger and reveal something about yourself, what you do for a living, what movie you saw last, what restaurant you ate in.

—Make a friend of someone you haven't met before. Try to find out if he/she is married, has children, is happy at work.

—Reveal something intimate about yourself to a new friend.

Each step requires a bit more risk, and each can be done on a different evening, but each time test your own reactions to see how anxious you get and how deeply you resist, what excuses you make. Be aware of what you feel inside when you are rejected or accepted, and examine how painful the rejection is. Can you live with the pain? If you can, try revealing a little more of yourself, and allow others to move closer to you. Be sensitive, not only to your own feelings, but to those of others.

No one has a monopoly on loneliness or rejection. The other person you relate to at the party may be hiding his insecurity behind a pseudointimatizer. Maybe you can reach out a helping hand to him or her.

Somebody Out There Loves Me

The young man is clean cut, well dressed, and overwhelmingly eager. He stops me on the street and asks, "How are you getting along with God these days?"

"I'm in a hurry," I answer.

"Is a moment too long for salvation?"

When I hesitate, considering the question, he says quickly, "You know, God loves you. He wants to save you. Can you share with Him and trust Him?"

Intrigued as I was by his use of the expressions *share* and *trust*, I still smiled and walked on. But I kept wondering, what had turned this young man to God for intimacy? A feeling of relationship with a spiritual being is a good thing, certainly. For many people, it can be a meaningful, important, and wonderful part of life. But in the last few years we have seen so many young people, unable to be intimate with their family and friends, turn to groups like the "Moonies," the "Jesus Freaks," the "Hari Krishnas."

Since that encounter I have talked and listened to a number of members of all of these groups. The message they preach has a sameness to it. *Jesus loves me. I can talk to Him. God cares. Krishna cares. I can trust God.*

These young people have found intimacy within a religion, something they could not find in the outside world. But perhaps they have also found a way of cutting themselves off from the hurt and rejection of that outside world. By doing this they have closed out the possibility of experiencing not only the joy, but the pain, of life. Can the love of God as well as the chanting fill an inner emptiness and alleviate an inner loneliness? Have they really discovered an inner meaning to life, or are they simply refusing to face reality?

Some psychologists see a similarity between these young people and the ones who go from one sensitivity group to another. Are they both searching for some tremendous involvement? Are they both motivated by a need to overcome alienation and loneliness? Religion can often provide an intimacy of its own to the true believer. It can be a part of life, not an escape or estrangement.

Compare the young convert I met in the street with Carol. She is an "encounter bum" and moves through the sensitivity circuit. On her last vacation she went out to Esalen, and before that it was a TM group in Brooklyn. She's been through EST and got "a fantastic amount out of Arica." Now she's looking into Primal Scream Therapy.

She will call me on Monday and tell me, "It was a wonderful weekend. The group was so close! I freaked out just looking into this girl's eyes. I felt free to touch. We were all friends."

Two weeks later she's off trying another group. The intimacy she found was momentary, illusive. It didn't last because there was no involvement after the weekend. Everyone was on a first-name basis—but few people asked for last names, telephone numbers, or addresses. They were able to be intimate for a few hours, knowing they were protected from any real involvement. They hid behind a cloak of anonymity.

Carol was afraid to risk involvement in a long-term relationship, and she used the encounter sessions to answer her need for intimacy. It was only because of Charlie, a young man she met one weekend at an encounter group, that she was able to break the pattern she seemed locked into.

What Carol had learned at the sessions wasn't bad.

In fact, on a one-to-one basis, the encounter techniques taught her to take a chance with Charlie. Through her friendship with Charlie, Carol began to understand that the weekend sessions had only been pseudointimatizers. Real intimacy came when she was able to trust and share with Charlie on a long-term basis.

The Self-Defeaters

Carol moved in encounter groups to block intimacy. Others find religion. There are many blocks to intimacy, and many different devices people use to achieve false intimacy. Unfortunately, they often spoil the very friendships they are after. Can you see yourself in any of these situations, as any of these people?

A hostile college professor cannot understand why his friends seldom invite him back a second time. He wants friendship, but he cannot trust anyone. He antagonizes others by using language as a battering ram against friend and stranger alike. He's always on the defensive and takes any position that allows him to discharge his hostility. The hostility defeats him by turning everyone off.

Then there is the eager beaver who plays the role of *accommodating fellow* or *self-sacrificing friend.* He is always available and nothing is too much to ask of him in the name of friendship. He wants to be used because he is convinced that he can only hold on to others by giving without asking in return. When his friends melt away he feels cheated and bitter. "I did so much for them. I never asked for anything."

The grabber's concept of friendship is "if you're my friend, you owe me something." Indebtedness is power. He sucks people dry with his demands. He is often a complainer and a bore, telling others all of his problems, but turning a deaf ear to theirs.

The demander phones and asks, "Why haven't you called me? It's been two days!" Intruding on everyone's private time and space, she not only makes demands, but she tries to take over the relationship. She wants to know everything about her friends, where they go, what they do, who they see. And she is jealous. She leaves no room for other relationships. Friendship must be exclusive.

The jealous lover demands and tries his best to get a relationship excluding all others. Lovers are best friends, and the myth says you can only have *one* best friend. Any other friendship that is close, caring, or loving becomes cause for jealousy. The jealous lover will make comments, like:

—What do you tell him about us?

—I think you care more about her than you do about me.

—Are you sleeping with him/her?

If you recognize yourself in any of these sketches, beware. You may want an intimate friendship, but you are setting up self-defeating blocks to it. Examine your relationships closely. Are you giving as much as you're trying to get? Are you giving too little, or too much? Intimacy must be based on mutual sharing as well as trust and empathy. Try putting yourself in the other person's position and discover how *you* would feel when you're faced with hostility, overaccommodation, a grabber, a demander, or a jealous lover.

There must be a fine balance in friendship, and with intimate friends there must also be caring and sensitivity to maintain that balance. What is acceptable behavior to one may be unacceptable to the other, and it's only through experiencing intimacy that we learn to accept and adjust and thus enrich our lives.

Hello, Good Buddy

William Safire, in an article in the *New York Times*, sees the rash of Citizen Band radios as a means of increasing intimacy among people unable to face each other. Like the darkroom, the CB radio lends a cloak of anonymity. The operator hides behind special "handles," *Good Buddy, Snow White, Big Mama, Betty Boop.*

Safire writes, "The lonely crowd wants company. A human being is not merely a receiver. Behind locked doors in cities, behind locked cliques in suburbs, behind locks of isolation in rural areas, individuals want to say—with no loss of safety or privacy—'Hello, I'm me. Let's talk about something.' "

As long as they have their CB radios turned on, the lonely crowd on our nation's highways, interstates, and backroads—drivers with little or no human involvement—can still feel a sense of friendship, a conviction that someone out there cares.

Television, that great filler of empty time, can give an illusion of some degree of intimacy, too, but in truth it's only a substitute for intimacy. A child may spend hours in front of the set, involving himself in an intimate relationship with the pictures projected on the tube. The child may see these images as people, but his intimacy with them is safe. It's one way to simulate relationships with people, except they can't talk back or order him around.

The adult too enjoys the same illusion. He also is intimate with the shadows. They become like old friends. Johnny Carson, Charlie's Angels, Rhoda, Kojak, all allow a viewer to enter their world and give him a sense of belonging. It expands his life, and no matter how unreal, it's still vivid and entertaining.

I don't want to criticize television too harshly because in many cases intimacy with the set is the only intimacy available. Friends on the tube are very real and important. They give a necessary illusion of involvement, an escape from despair and boredom and, most important, an offer of intimacy. Even if it's a substitute intimacy, it's all there is.

While, for some, television acts as a substitute, it's still only a visual substitute. Many people hunger for physical contact, and if they can't get it from other people, they turn to pets.

By the same token we are a nation of dog and cat lovers. Americans own over ninety million dogs and cats, and are willing to spend billions of dollars feeding them and caring for them. Industries have grown up based on our pet populations. We love these animals unreservedly, and we constantly anthropomorphize them, treating them not as animals but as humans. We use them to satisfy our desperate need for touch, for intimacy, for love.

A dog is a man's best friend. He'll love you no matter what you do to him, and he's always glad to see you. Can you say as much for your human friends? Can any of them give you the same unqualified love and acceptance?

I don't mean to imply that pets can't have a meaningful place in our lives. We can love them and care for them and use them as an intimate focus. What we shouldn't do is use a pet instead of a human to achieve intimacy *when a human is available.* In that case the pet satisfies a need that could be better satisfied by risking an involvement with a lover, friend, or relation.

I don't want to give the impression that loving and

caring for an intimate substitute is wrong. Even a small intimacy is better than none at all. We all long for a warm body, and if the only one available is that of a pet—why not take it?

Strangers in the Night

About twelve years ago, when my children and I were in the mountains for the summer, my husband was driving back to New York after a speaking engagement in Boston. It was late at night, and at a Thruway toll booth he picked up a bearded young man with a backpack trying to hitch a ride.

On the highway, in the darkness of the car, the young man and my husband began to talk, and within a very short time they had achieved a surprising degree of intimacy.

When my husband told me about it later, I commented. "You're very open with people. That's probably why he was able to be open with you."

"It was more than that," he told me thoughtfully. "The beard—that was the first thing. He was a kid who'd been given a hard time about that beard."

As they talked, the young man told my husband that he lived in Flint, Michigan, where he had gone to work in the auto factory straight from high school. He hated the assembly line work and didn't get on with the other workers who gave him a hard time about his hair. His family was just as unsympathetic. All they could see in him was *hippy*.

When he finally saved up a little money, he quit his job and took off to hitch around the country. As he put it, "I had to get my head together and find out what I wanted out of life."

It was very late when they got to New York, and he had no place to stay, so my husband offered him one of the kids' rooms to sleep in. "I guess I was taking a risk, but I felt that I knew him," my husband said. "We had become friends and I trusted him just as he trusted me—I guess it was the trust and sharing."

Two months later, my husband received a letter from the boy, the first of a series written over the years. My husband's young friend wrote that he was working in a music shop in Iowa, but was thinking of splitting for California. "I keep remembering our talk in the car. It sure meant a lot to me. I know you understood," he wrote.

It was a brief meeting, but an important one for the youngster. He risked revealing himself, not only to a stranger, but also to someone who was older. My husband too felt that he had gained more than he had risked that night.

In talking and thinking about the incident, I tried to put my finger on what had been responsible for the intimacy that both men felt that night. Was it just the act of revealing and sharing a problem? But if that was it, what factors had triggered it? For that matter, what factors go into making friends?

The first step in any kind of friendship is selectivity. Ask yourself, "Am I sure I want this person for a friend?"

The second step is to be aware of the depth of intimacy you want. How much of yourself will you share and reveal? Remember that you risk rejection, boredom, or too much involvement when you make that first move—but unless you make it there can be no intimate friendship.

The two most important factors in friendship are openness and acceptance. In essence, you say to any candidate for friendship, *I want to know you. I like you. I'm interested in you, and I'm going to let you know me.*

You can say all these things by sharing your private

feelings—the deeper the sharing, the more intimate the friendship will be. But you must also be wary of overwhelming your new friend. Share slowly, as the occasion arises.

The Safety of the Dark

I discovered another intriguing element to friendship when I read the account of a fascinating experiment done at several eastern colleges.

The experiment had been done with groups of college students between the ages of eighteen and twenty-five. The researchers' goal was to determine what happens to men and women in extremely anonymous conditions.

One group of students, four men and four women, all strangers, were put in a lighted room about ten by twelve feet in size. They were left to do whatever they pleased and they were photographed by concealed cameras.

A similar group was put in a similar room with absolutely no light. They too were photographed, but with invisible infrared light.

Both groups knew that there would be no system of rewards or punishments for their behavior, and they were told they would remain strangers after the experiment. The researchers wanted to see what people do to and with each other when they are cut off from the normal sanctions governing their lives.

"Will they do the usual social bit, or will they discover a new way of interacting?"

The controls, those students in the lighted room, came in, sat down—usually three feet apart—and stayed that way until the end of the session. While they were in the lighted room they kept talking and behaving much the way any group of students does in a new social situation. The lighted room experiment was run three times with much the same results.

The students in the dark room, on the other hand, behaved quite differently—in fact, quite shockingly! After thirty minutes, talk slackened and, unlike the students in the lighted room, these men and women began to roam around. Almost all of them touched each other intentionally, and half of the group hugged and kissed one another.

Asked to describe their impressions of that hour in the dark room, they talked of a feeling of closeness, a sense of friendship. Crawling over and around each other in the dark, they felt free, but also more serious than they usually did.

The researchers concluded that, deprived of light, perfect strangers could move quickly to a stage of intimacy that is often not reached in years of normal acquaintanceship.

Following these intriguing results, the researchers put another group of students into the dark room for a longer period of time, one hour and a half. During the last half-hour this group became even more open with each other, and talked about what they felt were "important things."

When you remove the visual aspects of an encounter, you are no longer risking judgment, and you cannot judge anyone else on purely physical grounds. This removes one of the biggest stumbling blocks in a relationship—physical standards and judgments.

We are all trained and conditioned to judge people physically. Has he a strong chin? He's dynamic. Is she pretty? She's sexy. Is he black? He's dangerous. Is he white? He's prejudiced—and so on. We absorb these stereotypes and there is a logical feedback when we meet someone and we react accordingly.

Remove all this and we are "little children stumbling in the dark," with all the accepting innocence of children. We are free to be open. Anonymity allows us to express our inner need to touch, and it encourages a deeper intimacy, both physical and psychological.

What the study indicates is the degree of inhibitions that exists when we come into social contact with others. Remove the inhibitions and you remove the barrier. We embrace intimacy the moment the inhibitions are removed—even with strangers.

The experiment also teaches us that a certain amount of mystery is desirable in intimate situations. We know that a "romantic setting," a candlelit table, soft lights, moonlit walks—any setting approaching darkness—increases intimacy.

Some of my most intimate memories of my brothers and sisters were long talks in the dark in our bedroom at night. My husband remembers nostalgically the intimacy of conversations after lights-out in a darkened tent at a summer camp.

One final observation we can draw from the lights-out experiment is that it demonstrates the overwhelming need, in all of us, for intimate closeness, both physical and psychological.

It is possible that, like the students in the experiment, all of us can come to know strangers in intimate moments. Without the protection of the dark we can still feel safe knowing we will probably never meet again. This can happen on planes, in buses, even on a park bench on a warm summer day. It can happen in a bar or in a restaurant in a strange city. The real trick is to learn to be intimate with those we continue to make contact with. And this can only be done by taking the risk.

Put Your Head on My Shoulder

We have talked so much about the risks we take when we become intimately involved with friends that it becomes clear that it is fear of risking that keeps people apart. What we must do to overcome that fear is to understand what an intimate friendship is.

Intimate friends must be tolerant of each other. We all know there is no perfect man or woman, and to expect perfection from a friend just isn't realistic. In friendship, along with the kindness and solicitude, there will also be pettiness, anger—even selfishness. We have to learn to accept these qualities.

But in accepting, we must understand that acceptance doesn't mean condoning or agreeing. Friends should disagree and argue too when they see differently. If there is genuine caring, sharing, and respect, one friend can understand what the other is saying without judging him.

Friendship cannot be narrowly defined. It is too wide in scope, and it encompasses too many aspects of feeling and emotion. The element of satisfaction is often the way intimacy in friendship is measured. If we feel unsatisfied because neither we nor our friends can share, then the friendship becomes casual and transitory.

There is satisfaction when we show caring and love for another person, and the satisfaction is deepened when the caring and love is returned. Often, one friend will be able to give more of himself than he receives, or one friend may have a greater need for emotional support. In a sense, we all trade off our abilities to take or give. It is only when the trade becomes one-sided that intimacy suffers.

I have spoken to hundreds of men and women about intimacy, and they all stressed the need to be themselves with their closest friends. Often they judged the closeness of a relationship by how secure they felt in it. I hear expressions like these again and again:

—I can let my hair down with her.

—I can be myself with him.

—He always has a shoulder ready for me to cry on.

—We feel good together, at ease, relaxed.

—I can tell my friend anything. He'll still care about me, and I can trust him with my secrets.

Learning to trust, learning to open ourselves to others, allowing them to trust us and be open to us—all takes time. Friendship must be worked at, must be given enough time to develop and grow. We have to be prepared to learn more about ourselves, in a friendship, even as we become more deeply involved with another.

There are many aspects of ourselves that we discover in our friends' eyes, and friendship can compel us to explore our inner selves more intensely than we ever did before.

Eleven

The Nine-to-Five Connection

A Double-Edged Knife

"You can talk about intimacy, but I'll tell you one place where you have to be damned careful about making friends, and that's on the job," Marvin told me. Marvin is an account executive with a small advertising firm. He makes a good living and enjoys his work. "I like people, and when my boss asked me to take this young guy under my wing, I said, 'Sure.' He seemed a nice, bright kid and he was eager to learn."

"What happened?" I asked.

"My wife Maggie says that I'm too trusting, but even she was taken in. We had him to the house for dinner and invited him out to the beach for the weekend. I listened to his problems, gave him advice about his girlfriend, and I clued him in to the working of my department, all the details.

"I thought we were friends. I trusted him and felt close to him and really cared about him. Then I found out that he was using me, playing on our friendship to take over my job. I tell you, I was knocked for a loop. My first reaction was hurt, and then I was sore as hell. Finally I was just plain scared. Hell, I'm over fifty, and here's this twenty-two-year-old pisher pushing to step into my shoes! I tell you, I'm too old to start with another firm."

"But you didn't lose your job?"

"I had to do some fierce infighting to hold on." Marvin continued, "I can't go through that kind of pain again, and it was pain! You invest a lot in an intimate friendship. Now I tell myself I'll never get that close to anyone I work with again." He laughed. "But what the hell. I can't live like that. I can't pull away from people and stop making friends because I'm afraid they'll knife me if they get a chance."

"What will you do?" I asked.

"I'll keep taking chances. For every bad apple there's a bushel of good ones. I've made an awful lot of friends in my time and I plan to make more."

Marvin's experience is similar to that of many people I've interviewed. He was aware, having been in the advertising business for years, that it was risky to confide in, to trust, to be too honest with another member of his work group. Yet, all he knew went out the window when a young man turned to him for guidance and friendship. In a highly competitive industry, Marvin has managed to stay a compassionate and decent person.

Intimacy in the nine-to-five world is a double-edged knife. It can cut both ways. Objectively it can be dangerous. An intimate friendship can be taken advantage of to get ahead. Subjectively the betrayal of a confidence, the discovery that someone you trusted, cared about, and were honest with, didn't level with you but used you, can make you less willing to take a chance in the future.

But it didn't work that way with Marvin, and the reason he was able to continue making friends was his sense of his own worth. He was good at his job and he knew it, and the knowledge gave him enough inner strength to get over the betrayal of his young friend and to continue making new friends.

Marvin's wife, Maggie, is an executive in an industrial management firm. She is very demanding in her choice of friends. "If I become friendly with anyone I work with, it's because I enjoy their company and feel comfortable with them. But in my office or out of it I'm picky, picky, picky about close friends!—and that's good." She hesitates. "But it's bad too."

"But you have a certain amount of power and prestige in your job," I say. "Don't you risk some of that when you get involved with a friend at work?"

Maggie agrees. "Yes. I move slowly until I'm sure the other person is being honest with me. It hasn't been easy getting to where I am now, but I did it on my own talent. I didn't use anyone and I didn't trade on friendship. I learned to value myself along the way. I think that's important."

"And your friends?"

She shakes her head. "I keep the option of deciding whether I want to get involved. In this job it would be foolish to form a close friendship with anyone under me. It just isn't done. In the same way I like my boss. He's interesting and fun, but it's not right for me to make friendly advances socially. I know it's a hell of a thing to say, but any friendship, casual or intimate, has to be examined in a realistic light."

Many of the people I spoke to about intimacy on the job were like Maggie—well aware that they faced many risks when they became intimately involved with their colleagues. Most were unwilling to take such a risk and they looked for close friends outside of work. There were others, however, who felt that they couldn't lock out the possibility of a new friendship that might have depth and meaning.

The Father Figure

I've known Adam for many years, and like Marvin he is open and makes friends easily. His attitude about life—and his job—is open and relaxed. When I talked to him and his young friend, Diane, they had just gone through a disturbing situation. Adam met Diane on the job. He was the editor of a trade magazine and she was the secretary of another editor on the same floor. It was a small company and there was a casual friendliness between most of the workers. "I always enjoyed young people," Adam said. "I got a kick out of Diane because she's alive and bright. For her part, I guess I was a father figure and that flattered me."

It was as a friend that Diane asked Adam if she could do an article for his paper even though she worked for someone else as a secretary. "I want to see if I can write," she said. "I don't expect to get paid, but I'd like you to criticize it."

Adam agreed and was delighted with the article she finally turned in. "You can write. I'll give you another assignment, and if it's as good I'll put through payment for you."

"It was then," Diane told me, "that it all hit the fan. My boss found out about Adam helping me, and he was furious. I had betrayed him! I was disloyal! I went behind his back! Why hadn't I come to him if I wanted to learn to write?

"I knew he would have refused to teach me because he wanted me as a secretary, but how could I tell him that? I didn't mean to be disloyal, but all he could understand was that I was *his* secretary, not Adam's. I was disloyal."

Diane was terribly hurt and in a vulnerable

position. She had no way of fighting back. It was easier for Adam because he was on her boss's level, but it was still messy. The other workers took sides and there was a lot of cruel gossip. But both Adam and Diane stood up to the gossip and remained friends. Bolstered by Adam's faith in her, Diane continued writing, and he, knowing she was good, kept going to bat for her. Eventually she left the company and got a new job working on a medical magazine, not as a secretary but as a junior writer.

"Was it all worth it?" I asked Adam and Diane at lunch one day.

"Absolutely!" Diane insisted. "Look, I learned a new skill and advanced myself, but best of all I made a good friend."

"I'll drink to that," Adam said. "A friendship like ours is worth the hassle we went through."

The Office Wife

The degree of intimate involvement between men and women who work together often depends on how much the man demands and how much the woman allows. It also depends on what each wants out of the relationship.

The office wife syndrome is typical of the secretary of the success-driven man who demands unswerving devotion and loyalty. What starts off as a boss-worker relationship gradually becomes more intimate and eventually takes on all the stereotypical overtones of a husband-wife setup.

The office wife is the caretaker wife away from home. She devotes her time, her energy, and her brains to her boss's needs, goals, and success.

The boss and his office wife may or may not have a sexual relationship as well, but the man knows that on any level of involvement she will not exploit his vulnerability. He feels safe enough to share his secret hopes and his innermost fears about the job.

She is more than a worker and even more than a wife because she becomes his empathic Rock of Gibraltar. Men who form such attachments, who make these unsigned contracts with their office wives, will often say, jokingly, "I'd sooner lose my wife than my secretary!"

But deep down the joke is deadly serious. Such devotion is hard to replace—a new wife is not usually as faithful as an old one.

The woman who takes on the role of office wife finds that her part of the unsigned contract answers many of her own needs. Often unmarried, she has channeled her desires to nurture and love into this office "marriage." Her own drive for recognition and power becomes tied up in the partnership, an intimate mix of sharing, vulnerability, and trust. This mix gives her an illusion of power and prestige. However, she is not all that different from her sister in marriage, the true wife who believes that only through her man can she gain recognition and importance.

A man and a woman working closely together do not have to make unsigned, one-sided contracts, to use each other for power and protection. There can be mutual trust and respect between them. Working together, cooperating on a project or being involved in the same field can cause a man and a woman to become supportive and trusting of each other. In working together, mutual feelings of respect and admiration can lay the groundwork for a truly intimate relationship without one-sided contracts.

Such relationships can sometimes grow and ripen into a genuine love that extends beyond the working intimacy. A sexual affair or even a marriage can develop. Two such people who come to intimacy in this way are less likely to exploit their nonworking relationship.

Both men and women, however, must be warned against the dangers inherent in an office wife/boss relationship. If you are involved in one, ask yourself these questions:

—Are you an older man who feels that life and age have caught up with you and now that your children are gone you and your wife have nothing in common?

—Do you feel that your job is a dead end and your life is wasted because you haven't fulfilled the desires and hopes of your youth?

—Are you convinced that this is your last chance to grab the brass ring of youth on the merry-go-round of life?

—As a woman, are you holding on to this relationship because you're afraid that if you let go you'll never get another chance?

—Are you comfortable enough in your job, or couldn't you get along without your office wife?

—How long have you waited for that commitment of his, that promised divorce, marriage, or whatever? Is it a matter of years?

—Does the sexual involvement with your boss give you a sense of power and control?

—Do you feel that if you left your job tomorrow, he couldn't manage without you?

If you can answer yes to any one of these questions, then you must take another close look at your relationship. The chances are that one of you is using the other and that there is no real possibility of intimacy.

Consenting Adults

The risk of sexual involvement between men and women who work together is very real. The entire thing can end in an intimate relationship, or it can turn into an emotional and economic disaster.

In a working situation, it is usually the woman who is in the vulnerable position and can be hurt more easily. She runs the risk of not only emotional damage but also economic reprisal, for it is she who is usually in the less important job and is easier to replace. She is also the one to become the target of gossip and rumor. The general feeling is, *she asked for it.*

Her male partner gets off with, *he's human. Any guy will take what he can get. She didn't have to get involved. She could have said no.*

If the woman is married and has children, she's doubly condemned, but for the married man with a family—*most married men play around, given the chance.*

We give lip service to the consenting adult morality, but there is still a decided prejudice against the working woman and office sex. The entire theory of *consenting adults,* as far as sexual behavior in the working world is concerned, has been exploded. In a recent massive survey, *Redbook* Magazine polled 9,000 working women between eighteen and sixty years of age in terms of how they handled sex on the job. The majority were married and in their early twenties and thirties.

Most of the women worked at white collar jobs, but there was a good-sized group of professionals and many blue collar workers. In all, it was a survey that covered women of almost every age and class.

There was unanimous agreement that sex was indeed alive on the job front, but not always well. There was a great deal of sexual exchange, and often it was enjoyable without being threatening. However, most women felt that at some period in their working lives they had to put up with unwelcome and upsetting sexual contacts.

Is this something new? Obviously not, since many of the women reported that it had gone on for years. What is new is that now they feel free enough to talk about it. It used to be considered too embarrassing, too trivial, too threatening to mention.

Ninety-two percent of the women surveyed stated that sexual harassment on the job was a problem. The range of harassment covered everything from sexual remarks, leering, and touching to outright demands for sex.

The most frequent kind of harassment reported was verbal, either a comment on a woman's body, a dirty joke, or a description of sexual positions and acts.

" 'Sticks and stones can break my bones but names can never hurt me' must have been written by a man," a woman told me angrily. "That's the out the guys use when you confront them with your annoyance. Or else they pretend they are paying you a compliment—some compliment, to have your breast size discussed around the water cooler, or have to listen to the intimate details of your boss's sex life! If you get mad, you can be out of a job, or your anger is taken as a big joke. It's all in the name of kidding around and teasing. So you shrug it off and pretend it doesn't affect you, but I tell you—sometimes I feel as if I'm being raped by words. He's getting off on my embarrassment, and I feel angry and ashamed!"

The physical assault, invading a woman's private space and touching her body, are included in the second most common form of sexual harassment on the job. Most working women have experienced some form of pinching, grabbing, touching, brushing, stroking, patting—even goosing. Nine out of ten times it is unwanted, and yet it often escalates into an open demand for sex. A friend tells me that two of the men in her office are nicknamed the *Gross Grabbers*. "They could give lessons to subway molesters," she declares. "They are always just accidentally brushing against me or bumping into me."

In all fairness, men are not always the ones at fault. The reverse side of the coin is that in the *Redbook* survey, thirty percent of the women admitted using their sexual attractiveness to get ahead on the job, and many of the women said they felt they had been passed over in favor of less competent workers who were willing to be more cooperative sexually.

How can sexual put-downs, overt passes, and outright sex demands be managed on the job? It's a tough question that deserves a tough answer. The unwanted verbal or physical intimacy can be faced, and, whenever possible, should be faced in an assertive manner. In spite of the risk to her job, if a woman remains silent and endures even small indignities she becomes powerless and loses a part of her own self-respect.

The first step in handling sexual harassment at work is to become aware of what is actually taking place, and to understand your inner reactions of anger, embarrassment, or shame. Why shame? Because women have been too quick to place the blame on themselves.

"It's my fault that he talked to me that way. I guess my skirt was too short—or maybe I did something to lead him on."

The second step is to assess the situation honestly. What was your initial reaction to the harassment? If you really were responsible, if you were sending out the wrong signals, then you must take the responsibility. But if the fault isn't yours, it may be time to decide whether it's worth risking some assertion in order to keep your own sense of dignity and integrity.

A good example of someone successfully risking assertion was told to me by a young physiotherapist working at her first job in a small hospital. She looked young for her age, pretty and petite, but she was good at her job.

"I didn't play the little girl role," she told me, "but Dr. Gordon, the chief of our division, treated me like a child. He'd single me out and say, 'You're doing beautifully, sweetheart. This is a hard job for a pretty little kid." Then he'd give me a Big Uncle pat on the head. He meant well, but he was condescending and I was embarrassed. I had to do something before I blew my cool!"

The young woman handled the situation with wit and assertion. Arranging to see the doctor in his office, she used a calm, friendly voice to tell him she was disturbed about the way he treated her, but she was uneasy about bringing it up.

He was genuinely bewildered. "What's troubling you?"

"I know you interned here many years ago," she said seriously, "and I wondered if, when you were an intern, your chief showed his approval by patting you on the head and telling you it was a hard job for a young kid."

There was a long silence, and the young woman could feel her heart pounding. Had she risked too much? Had she gone too far, been too forward? The doctor was shocked, but after a moment he began to laugh. "I get the picture. I think my family's right. I'm a male chauvinist!"

The young woman joined in his laughter. She had made her position clear and she had kept not only her job, but a good working relationship, and most important, her own self-esteem. Things were better after that.

But not all sexual harassments are that light and can be handled with humor and good will.

Sometimes you cannot wait to talk the problem over. You have to confront your harasser immediately. "Watch out for Powell," an older woman cautions a young worker in an electronics plant. "He tries to get all the women in the back of the stockroom."

The new worker asks, "How do you handle him?"

"I stay out of his way or I ignore him."

The new woman is not as easily intimidated as her older friend, and when Mr. Powell brushes up against her for the first time, she moves away and says, firmly, "Please don't do that. I don't like it."

He retreats with a disarming grin. "Just an accident. Don't be so touchy."

"I think you're the one who's touchy," she answers quickly. When it happens again, she's ready. "Look, Powell. I feel uncomfortable when you accidentally touch me. I like you and I like this job—but I don't like this game. Okay?"

The ball is in his court and he has to make a decision. Should he stop the sexual game or risk an issue being made about it? In the end he takes the easy way out and stops annoying her.

This forthright confrontation is an exception. Generally, women tend to play it safe. They are not the risk takers that men are. They still feel too vulnerable on the job, but as long as they fear speaking out, they will continue to be vulnerable to sexual harassment.

Each working woman must decide for herself what risks are worth taking and which are not. In turn, when men stop seeing women in terms of sexual use, they can begin to see them as human beings in an intimate, friendly, or working relationship. On or off the job, the intimate future of men and women lies in being friends and colleagues, in mutual respect, trust, and sharing.

Moving Out

Intimate friendship implies a sense of commitment, and there is a correlation between commitment and the duration of a friendship. In a society like ours, where there is tremendous job mobility, most people do not want to invest too much emotion or feeling in a relationship that is likely to be short termed.

Gary, Sylvia, and Harold work in the same company on different levels. All three are in the process of moving out of their particular work group. Harold's move is the most traumatic of the three. He has been demoted and he knows it is time to start looking for another job.

At forty-eight, Harold has been in his department for twelve years, and many of his colleagues are friends—a few are very close friends. They get together socially and they often lunch together or have a drink after work.

Two years ago, when Harold's closest friend, Al, needed money, Harold loaned it to him. When Harold's oldest boy was accepted in medical school, both families celebrated together. Inevitably, Harold turned to Al when the ax fell. "I'm looking for another job."

Al's reaction was shock and dismay. "My God, you've been here longer than any of us. You can't leave now!"

Harold shook his head. "I knew it was coming and it's impossible for me to stay. They didn't come right out and fire me, but they want to move me down with a cut in pay. I couldn't take that, so I handed in my notice."

That weekend Al insisted that they get together and have a drink and talk. But as the days go by and Harold begins to wind up his life at the office, there is a noticeable change as the other workers begin to separate themselves from Harold, and he in turn moves away from them.

The intimacy he felt with his friends, the seeming closeness that was a part of the work group, has evaporated. "They all avoid me like the plague," he tells his friend, Al. "They pretend to care, but all they're really worried about is their own skins. I think it's a mistake to make friends at work."

"Well, it's worked out for us," Al shrugged. "We're still good friends."

"Well, we're different."

"Maybe, but I'll tell you, Harold, some of the other guys would have stuck with you if you had let them."

Harold thought about that a moment. "Maybe, but the point is, you were the only one I thought I could trust. I think we're really friends."

"I'll shake on that," Al smiled.

Moving Up

Gary's situation is different. He's leaving the group because he's moving up the corporate ladder. He has few emotional ties to the people he works with, but he has always masked this lack with a pretense of friendship. He seems to be interested in those who work with him. He does the right things in a social way, but he has deliberately avoided any real involvement with anyone on an intimate level. He is ready to move, to break ties, to cut off friendships at a moment's notice. His emotional bags are always packed.

Like many upwardly mobile wives, Gary's wife is expected to follow her husband's example. If it is useful, pretend an involvement or an intimacy, but don't let yourself get too close to anyone, or trust them too much. Don't allow yourself to feel deeply about another person.

Gary manages very well. As soon as he knows he is going to become a vice president in the firm, he begins to shed his junior executive role. He drops all his old friends, and there is a period of isolation before he makes new ones.

What destroyed all of Gary's careful planning was the unprecedented promotion of a man, formerly under him, to a position above him. He had snubbed the man when his friendship wasn't worth much to him. Now, in turn, the man would not allow Gary's friendly overtures. Gary was forced to take a second look at his own actions. Had it been worthwhile avoiding intimacy?

Moving Sideways

Sylvia is the third worker involved in a move. Unlike Gary or Harold, she is moving laterally. The company is transferring her within the firm, but her new position will be in their out-of-town office. Her new job will be much the same as her old one, and there will be no increase in salary.

On the friendship and intimacy level, Sylvia worries that her friends may reject her. The women in her steno pool have always had a nice camaraderie, and Sylvia has made some close and enduring friendships among them. Now, with the uncertainty of motives about her transfer, the women in the pool become uneasy. They feel a reflection of Sylvia's anxiety, and when the rumors and gossip begin, they take sides. One group feels that transfer is a step down. Another, smaller group, feels it's definitely a step up—but each group is re-evaluating their feelings about Sylvia. If she is taking a step up, they see her as a more important person, a person to stay friendly with. If it's a step down, then she is on her way out, a failure, and since failure is contagious, they may catch it.

Two of her close friends manage to stay in touch with Sylvia. Both of them see her not just in terms of her job and performance, but as a whole person. They want to keep the relationship they have built up over the past years. As she trains a new secretary to take over her old job, she is filled with mixed emotions. She sees her replacement moving into the group and gradually being accepted, and she wonders whether she should get too friendly with anyone in her new job. The pain of leaving, of being replaced, is too devastating.

But the comfort of her two close friends reassures her. They help her move and give her a going-away lunch and in general make life easier for her at this rough period. Sylvia realizes that although she has held several jobs in the past ten years, she has come away from each job with at least two or three close intimate friends.

Her vulnerability at having to leave the job has made her forget this, but now, with all that these friends do to help, she realizes that intimate friends are rarely lost—and always worth making.

The Interchangeable Man

The average person in this country does the job he has to do, regardless of what he wants to do. The expectations of youth, before they enter the work force, are often unrealistic. They become only daydreams when the young person finds that in order to make a living he must work at a dull, routinized job. The American dream of freedom of choice remains, for many of us, just a dream.

The assembly line worker epitomizes the complete lack of involvement between man and job. He never completes a task. The car chassis goes by and he tightens a bolt. Another chassis—again the same gesture. He is an interchangeable cog, and he gives up any sense of fulfillment or worth in work—any feeling of intimacy with his job.

Can he turn to others in the same boat to establish an intimate friendship? Many firms and factories, realizing the need for this, attempt to give the workers intimacy by methods such as a coffee break. This provides a momentary escape from work to allow social contact with others. The little flirtations, the joking, the exchange of gossip all serve as a small bolster to self-esteem.

When there is little or no intimate involvement with job or colleague, the search for satisfaction must be directed elsewhere. Often, the blue collar worker can find it within his family. This is particularly true if his family is intimate and loving and can survive, intact, when the going gets rough.

The Workaholic

At one end of the job spectrum are those interchangeable workers who feel little involvement in their jobs. They number in the millions. A much smaller group lies at the other end of the job spectrum. They are the workaholics, a recent term coined to describe people who are so completely involved in their work that they find no time or energy for intimate relationships.

Workaholics are men who are driven to succeed. Now, however, more and more women are joining the club. Most workaholics have set themselves the goal of making it before thirty. They set timetables and goals for success, but once they succeed they are only driven to work harder, to spend more time and more energy seeking more success. They have to make *it*, and *it* means not only money but acceptance into a privileged, elite group in business, the professions, or politics.

Often the workaholic nurtures that part of his personality which is highly competitive and selfish. He cherishes emotional detachment and coldness, and puts a low premium on intimacy. Understanding, empathy, trust are all emotions he can do without. He is a man, or she is a woman, not afraid of risking if the risk involves a chance of more power or success. But if the risk is on a personal level, toward intimacy, he avoids it.

The workaholic makes a tremendous show of company loyalty, but he is really committed only to himself, and he defines that self in terms of superachievement. He cannot afford to worry about failure or what a move may mean to his family.

It often happens that a man with all this drive and aggressiveness will abdicate power within his own family. He makes a poor husband and father because he is so intimately involved with his success drive. There is no time for intimacy with anyone in the family.

Scratch the surface of such a man—or woman—and you will find a vulnerable child afraid to be found out and held up to ridicule. His vulnerability drives him to fill his time with work.

There's little that can be done for the workaholic without intensive psychiatric help. Work addiction is like any other addiction and is just as difficult to cure. But we can look to the future and try to prevent our own children from falling into this pattern.

What makes such a man a workaholic? According to some psychiatrists it is an overbearing mother and an absent or weak father, the same forces, incidentally, that they feel are responsible for male homosexuals.

Intense poverty or prejudice can also contribute to making a workaholic. So can a parent who is determined that the child will have all the opportunities the parent missed.

Money and all it means is secondary to workaholics. They must have it, but they don't particularly enjoy using it. The main drive is to get to the top of the heap—and intimacy along the way is only an anchor to hold them down.

The Independents

The old dream of starting a small business, of being independent and your own boss, is rooted deeply in the American culture. It is a dream that belongs to the early 1880s when many Americans were able to stand on their own feet in small businesses, farms, and ranches throughout the country.

The dream has very little reality for most of us today, and yet there are many who still cling to it. The man struggling to maintain a small grocery in the face of the supermarkets, the woman with a little dress shop near a department store, the one-man ad agency struggling to keep afloat are all looking for something more than financial success. They are caught up in the dream that as long as they are their own bosses they also keep some control over their lives.

"Sure we work long hours. We have to keep our heads above water," the wife of the grocery store owner tells me. "It's a matter of self-respect," her husband adds. "I keep that by being my own boss."

"I know who I am. I'm not another guy to be

pushed around by the art director. I'm my own man," the small ad agency owner tells me.

"Maybe I don't sell what Gimbels does," the woman in the small dress shop says, "but I'm using my own talent. No one else is using me to get rich!"

The need for identity and self-respect is tied to the dream of independence. If you are your own boss, you are not replaceable or interchangeable. You are not just a cog in that vast machine. You have value to yourself and to your work.

When you've reached that stage of self-esteem, you are able to reach out to others in an intimate fashion. You are worth something to yourself, so you must be worth something to them.

These independent people have an intimate involvement with the work they're doing. I found that same involvement, on a slightly different level, among artists, writers, and craftsmen. A woman poet in San Francisco told me, "I write for myself. It's an intimate act. My words, my feelings make the poem. I feel an affinity, a closeness with the writing. It's a deep personal part of my being. It isn't a piece of work I grind out for someone else."

"But how do you make enough to live?" I ask her.

"I teach and sometimes I lecture. I enjoy both and I'm involved with them up to a point, but not as intimately as I am with my poetry. I'm always aware that I have to conform to rules in the school. I'm doing a job for someone else and it's a way of making a living."

Several months after I spoke to her, I talked to a painter in New England about intimacy and work. Of all the creative people I spoke to, he was the most articulate.

"It's *my* work," he told me. "*I'm* responsible for it. I put myself on the line each time I take up a brush." He paced around his studio restlessly. "Intimate? My God, it's so damned intimate!"

Creative people as a group, I found, were able to maintain a good deal of control over their work. They created a book, painting, song, a piece of pottery out of their own ideas, experiences, intellect, and emotions. Their creation was something they carried through from inception to completion.

Some of them became so intimately involved with their work that they turned away from others for long periods of time, often isolating themselves from the pressures and demands of even close family relationships. For most of them, however, the intense involvement with their work, the joy of creativity and the freedom of expression enhanced their ability to share, to be warm and compassionate—to be more intimate—with their families and friends.

But most important of all, creative people learn—if their creativity is to be meaningful—to risk within the framework of their art. They can, very often, carry this ability to risk, to take a chance, to move out of a rigid framework into their personal lives.

Often, this risking is frowned on by society. Artists, in risking, tend to make their own rules, to be the Bohemians of their times. But taking a risk or a chance, breaking the rules, is what risking is all about.

The defensive question, "I am not creative so how can I do it?" must be answered by the fact that there is creativity in all of us. Recognizing and realizing that creativity is a step toward maturity.

Twelve

The Pain of Parting

The Fear of Dying

In the last chapters we considered separation and its impact on intimacy. In a work situation, moving not only affects the mover, but also those who remain. Often, the emotional upheaval of such a situation is, in a minor key, similar to the emotional upheaval of death.

The Device of Denial

On an emotional level, dying is separation, withdrawal, and even desertion. The survivors are left with an irreplaceable loss, and sometimes they cannot face up to it. Rudy's wife was like that, only she couldn't even face the certainty of her husband's death.

Rudy was a friend of mine from school whom I hadn't seen in many years. I met him by chance on the street about a year ago, and after I asked him the usual routine questions: "How are you? What are you doing now? How many kids do you have?" we decided to have a cup of coffee together and catch up.

In my kitchen, I started to put the coffee on. I was telling Rudy about the book I was writing when he dropped his bombshell. "I have a story for you about intimacy."

"Good. Should I take notes?"

He shook his head. "I think you'll remember. Last year I discovered I had leukemia. Six months later my wife left me." He said these words very quietly, matter-of-factly.

I turned back to the stove, the coffee pot in my hand, fighting a sudden sense of vertigo. He waited till I recovered enough to sit down, then he went on. "I know it's a bummer, and this is a hell of a way to break the news."

"I'm so sorry!" I said, even though I couldn't hide the shock in my voice.

"It was hard enough to realize the truth and face up to it," Rudy went on as we sat there, "but what was really devastating was that my wife Stella couldn't take it. I tried to tell her about my anxiety and fear, but she just wouldn't let me talk about it.

"I realized then that we hadn't really been intimate for years, and now, when I needed someone, there was no one to turn to. It wasn't just Stella. The fault was mine too. At the time I hadn't been close to anyone—friends, my kids, my family . . ."

Rudy told me how he had denied to himself that he was going to die, then how he was deeply angry at the unfairness of it all, and finally how he accepted it.

"No man should know his own death, but I had been given a timetable. I have chronic leukemia with eight to ten years to live."

"It must be frightening," I murmured.

"It was, and sad too, but something happened that changed me. Accepting death gave an immediacy to my life. I realized there was so much I wanted to do, to say—each day was filled with such intensity. I was really alive for the first time in years.

"I wanted to share that realization with Stella, but she backed away from that much intimacy—with a dying man."

"Perhaps it was too painful for her," I suggested.

"Perhaps. She just didn't want to listen. Her attitude was 'We'll go on the way we have been and maybe in a few years they'll discover a cure.' But I didn't want to go on as we had. I wanted more. I wanted to know what she was really thinking and feeling, all her fears and terrors. They would have helped me dispel my own."

"What happened?"

He shrugged. "She ran away, clear across the country. At first she said she wanted to visit her folks for a while, but then she wrote and made it clear she wasn't coming back."

"And your children?"

"They're married and they have their own lives, but I'm closer to them now than I was in all the years they were growing up. I'm able to open up to them and share the good and the bad about dying. They're great kids.

"If there's anything positive about this, it's that I feel more alive now than I have in years. It's not a drug euphoria. For the first time in my life I'm in touch with myself and involved with life. If I'd met you on the street a few years ago I'd have said hello and that would have been that. I would never have risked opening myself up this way."

"And now?"

"Well, I take all kinds of chances. If I love someone, I tell them so. If I want to see someone, I see him. I'm alive."

After Rudy left, I realized that in the few hours we had just spent together I had come to know him as a friend. He had revealed and shared a private, intimate part of himself. His impending death had freed him to take the risk, but when he asked his wife to share his risk, he lost her. She left in an effort to protect herself from her own feelings.

Unfortunately such protection only works on a short-time basis. It's predictable that when Rudy dies, her unresolved anger, anxiety, and love will catch up with her. The ambivalent feelings she has bottled up inside will explode into unbearable grief and eventual guilt.

Stella used the device of denial to handle her husband's impending death. We all use devices of one sort or another to cope with our fears of death. But when we use denial to cope with these fears, we become the victim of our inner conflicts and anxieties.

In retreating from this most intimate part of life, we are saying that it is better not to feel than to feel pain. The truth, however, is that it's far better to feel the bad with the good than to experience that most terrible desolation of all—no emotions.

In writing about the paradoxes of love, Rollo May explains that the awareness of death gives us an intensified openness to love. Rudy's own story is a confirmation of that thought. But many of us will find some device to avoid the pain of separation and death.

There are those people for instance, who carefully avoid loving too much, becoming too intimate even with their own children as well as their lovers simply because they are terrified of death and all its ramifications of desertion and loss. They settle for lives of minimum feeling and involvement. When, in spite of this, they are faced with the reality of death, they cannot cope.

"I never visit sick friends," one woman declared. "Hospitals and sickness depress me!" The anger in her voice was as revealing as her words. What she was really saying was, "I cannot bear to be intimate with someone who will leave me."

Another person, a middle-aged man, defended his reasons for not attending his brother's funeral. "Funerals don't mean anything. I sent flowers and I'll help out his family." The truth is his own fears of death are so overwhelming that attending the funeral would be like rubbing his nose in his own mortality!

A friend told me that after he had suffered a severe heart attack, his friends and his family had trouble looking at him when they came to visit in the hospital. "They would come in," he said, "glance at me and then look away. I knew I looked awful, but my God! I was still alive. I was still me!"

Another woman had a happier experience dealing with a loved one, although initially there were barriers. She was suffering from a dangerous staph infection after surgery. Her father came to see her every day. "He never talked much, and I thought he was coming only out of a sense of duty. In two minutes he'd have the television on. It bothered me. Didn't he know how sick I was, or didn't he care? Then the night nurse said something that made me think.

" 'Your father loves you,' she said. 'He just doesn't know how to tell you. He hides behind the television set.' "

"I don't know how to talk to him either," she admitted to the nurse. "I wish I could let him know how frightened I am."

"Why not try saying it," the nurse suggested.

The next afternoon, before her father could turn on the television, she said, "Come over here and sit on my bed. I just want you to be with me. I love you, and I need you now." She went on to tell her father how terrible the last weeks had been and how close to death she still felt she was.

He took her hand and sat on the bed. "I'll be here," he said slowly. "I've been frightened too. I've prayed for you every day." He made no move toward the television set then or on any other visit.

That moment, she told me, was the breakthrough for both of them. They both felt a tremendous feeling of relief and later it became possible for them to talk, to really communicate and to cope with her illness. "I was close to death and we both knew it and talked about it, and we comforted each other."

Letting go emotionally freed her to express her love for her father. It also allowed her to talk about her anxiety, grief, and fears that she wouldn't survive the illness. For someone facing death, this verbal expression of inner fear and doubt becomes a necessity. It's also necessary for someone who loves that person to share those fears and doubts.

Denying or avoiding these honest emotions is equivalent to saying, "I don't want to be intimately involved. I don't want to hear about your fears or face my own." Such a reaction is a cruelty.

Companioning into Death

The husband of a young woman I had known handled her coming death in an extremely sensitive, intimate way. Milly had terminal cancer and a limited time to live. Together, she and her husband Leo decided that she would spend as much of that time as she could with her family. When she felt well enough, she prepared dinner and helped the children with their homework. When she needed help from them, she asked for it. She even compiled a list of clothing they would need for summer camp, though she might not still be alive to see them go.

"It will be a part of me that's still around," she told her husband.

The list, the plans for camp, the long talks with her husband about the children and their future were a comfort to her. "Milly was a truly remarkable person," her husband told me. "I always knew that she valued herself, even when she was so ill. There was a sense of integrity about her."

But Milly could never have let her family accompany her to death without a husband who was willing to be intimate, to share the pain and sorrow of dying.

"I'll never forget the experience," he told me after her death. "What impressed me most was that Milly was in charge of her life, even when she was dying. I was impressed by that and the wonderful intimacy between us. Neither of us was afraid to say what we really felt, even the sad things."

In her book *On Death and Dying* Dr. Elizabeth Kubler-Ross and her staff found that out of two hundred terminally ill patients only one didn't want to talk about the seriousness of her illness or her fear of dying. Most patients were well aware of just how ill they were, but often they could not share this knowledge or their fears with those closest to them. They wanted to talk—in fact they needed to, but the message they got from family and friends was *don't mention such painful things.*

The ill and dying do not want to play the game of superficial conversation. Dr. Kubler-Ross found this to be clear again and again. The dying patients she interviewed emphasized that they wanted to share their concerns and feelings, especially their feelings of anger, rage, envy, guilt, and isolation. They wanted, indeed desperately needed, intimacy.

If it is not the dying who are afraid to be intimate, it is the survivors who are. How then should we deal with the terminal illness of someone we love? How should we deal with our own impending death?

First we must come to terms with ourselves and our own feelings about death. We are all aware that we exist and that we will die someday, but few of us can look at our own death objectively. The idea of non-being terrifies us. Like infinity, we know that non-being exists, but emotionally we cannot comprehend it.

Coping by denial, by avoiding any thought of dying, by attempting to close off our inner feelings, only serves to intensify our fears. The energy we spend in running away from death would be much better spent in living.

We must cope with the idea of death by accepting it, although not by dwelling on it. While we are alive we must be intimately involved with living, and this means being intimately involved with others. Intimacy right up to death is our greatest tool for coping with it. Most of us have had no experience with death and dying. We know little about the emotions of a person near death, and there is no one who can tell us what happens after death.

Changing life styles keep the extended family apart, and old age, illness, and dying are all tucked away in sanitary nursing homes and hospitals. Our culture insists that it is easier, less threatening, and less painful to separate death from feeling. The message is clear. *Don't be involved. Don't think. Don't feel.*

In spite of this, death surrounds us. We are a society that deals in death, but it is a death without emotion. Death on the television screen is not the same as the personal death of someone we love. Death by body count or catastrophe is seen on the news, but not intimately absorbed. We are able to deny it by simply switching channels or by saying it won't happen to us.

But when we are suddenly faced with the death of someone we love, we are not equipped to deal with the painful and frightening emotions it arouses. We push them down and cover them up.

We must learn to face death, to understand that it is a natural part of life, and inevitably it must come to all of us. There are rewards to being intimately involved with it. When we can handle the emotions surrounding it and admit the pain and loss we feel, we will discover in ourselves some of the most wonderful and gratifying human emotions—compassion, kindness, understanding, unselfishness, and love.

In study after study of dying people, researchers found that the dying wanted the companionship of those they loved. They didn't want to be isolated or left to die alone. Indeed, when no family or friends were available, dying people would risk intimacy with nurses, fellow patients, attendants—anyone who showed concern and caring.

When people are close to death, they need to talk about the fears and anxieties that they attach to death. After the tragic accident in the spring of 1977 when two jumbo jets collided on the runway in the Canary Islands, most of the survivors were flown to hospitals in the United States. These people had gone through a terrifying experience and had been forced to face death. Many were suffering not only from shock, but from serious injuries and burns. All of them coped, not by blocking out the horror, but by facing it and talking about it. They needed to talk and, in a sense, to relive the entire experience.

My daughter writes to me about her own reactions to death and dying in a hospital in the midwest where she works with elderly people.

"One of the greatest needs of the elderly or dying person," she said, "is to be touched. A simple stroke of the head or shoulder, a willingness to hold hands, will do it.

"Death is a lonely time, a time of desertion, and while many older people accept death, they still feel alone and removed from the outside world. They are often too proud to risk reaching out for love, and so they deny their need."

In writing about how she coped, she said, "I love to ask old people about the early years of their life. I am genuinely fascinated by a world before electricity or automobiles and planes and they delight in my fascination. I love to ask the women for recipes, to share a family cake or pie with me, and they respond.

"We learn to turn away from poverty and ugliness, and in the same way we turn away from illness and pain, thinking that if we don't see it it won't affect us. But inevitably it does. It's a vital part of us. We must confront death and let the dying know that we, the living, suffer emotionally as they suffer physically."

Thirteen

Take a Chance with Intimacy

Between Thumb and Finger

Throughout our lives, we carry certain hidden vulnerabilities with us. Let me be intimate with you and share a very painful one. My family was not a very intimate one. My mother was usually too harried and busy with five children to pay much attention to any one of us. By nature she was not a demonstrative woman.

Perhaps because of this I longed to be touched and held, to be assured in words and actions that I was loved. I remember her sitting at the kitchen table shelling peas one summer afternoon. Leaning up against her knee, I asked, "Mama, do you love me?"

"Don't lean on me, dear. I'm very busy now." This should have been indication enough of how she felt.

But I persisted. "Do you really love me, Mama?"

Pushing me away, and with her eyes still on her work, she said, "Of course." This was my first lesson in ECP—extra communication perception.

"How much?" I asked anxiously.

She looked down at me with a sigh of exasperation. Then she held her hand close to my face, her thumb and forefinger pressed together. "Can you see through that?"

I peered anxiously at the fingertips, but I could see no light between them. I asked her the same question later that day and got the same answer—thumb and forefinger pressed together with no ray of light shining through to indicate the depth—or shallowness—of her love.

To her it was an affirmation of love, but it was devastating to me. I stopped asking. The hurt and the rejection were too much to bear at five years of age.

Years later, my husband said to me, "Why is it so hard for you to tell me you love me?"

"Don't be silly," I answered guiltily at first. "I'm just not as demonstrative as you are. My family background—we never showed emotion."

"Try it now."

"All right," I said, noting that suddenly my lips were dry. "I love you!"

I must have looked stricken because he added softly, "How do you feel when you say it?"

"Awful! I have this terrible fear that you'll laugh at me."

And then I remembered my mother's thumb and forefinger pressed too tightly together when I asked for love. Had I resolved then never to ask for love again? Was I still afraid to commit myself? That fear of being rejected must still be with me!

It is that same fear of rejection that makes it hard for all of us to take that final step, to declare ourselves, to expose ourselves, to be vulnerable.

We all learn to risk—or we learn how terrible risking can be—while we are still children. I learned my own vulnerability before I could learn to understand it. Fortunately, as I grew older, I took risks simply because I so desperately wanted the intimacy I had been denied as a child. I came to learn that intimacy is not a static thing. Our need for it changes as our life changes.

Other children, no matter how they want that intimacy, may be too vulnerable to ask for it—or, asking for it early in life, they may find that what they get is not worth the pain.

In writing *Getting Close* I went through a re-evaluation of my own intimate feelings, and my intimate relationships with others. Out of necessity I learned how to listen in interviewing people, even friends and family. I discovered that most people want to be intimate. They need to know that they're being listened to, that someone cares enough to listen.

Too often people listen to others only to get their own opinions in. If you are to open yourself to intimacy, then you must learn to *really* listen, even to the point of withholding your reaction. You must not only listen to someone, but you must feel genuine concern for them, and for their problems.

Most of the people I talked to told me about *their* lack of intimacy, *their* needs, *their* desires, *their* abortive emotional lives, *their* struggle to find love—and always the emphasis was on *themselves*.

Listening to others, talking to them, I became aware that a prime concern was with ourselves—and yet we claim we wanted to be intimate with someone else. Our society stresses self-fulfillment and independence, competition, achievement, and power, and, up to a point, all of these qualities are valuable. But when the *I* comes first, as in "*I want, I need, I demand,*" then intimacy becomes an impossibility. Self-indulgence replaces respect, exploitation replaces love, and mutual caring is locked out.

If you want trust, you must give trust. If you want love, you must be able to love back. In psychotherapy, sacrifice, unselfishness, and tolerance are values that are too often scorned. Kindness, compassion, and affection are seen as psychological weaknesses, when actually they are the bulwark of close and caring relationships.

A truly intimate pairing between two people has many different aspects. On one level it is an interlocking, an adjustment of two people to a single unit. The unit must function together, must be at ease with itself and—most important of all—must be separate when necessary.

Paradoxically, every good, intimate relationship, whether between friends, families or lovers, embodies separation. Each individual is just that—an individual, a unique person with his own desires and needs. Sometimes those desires and needs match those of a partner, and sometimes they don't. Sometimes they even conflict.

When two people's needs don't correspond, or when they conflict, there must be mutual respect for the other's opinion and a realization that such respect will not affect either party's self-esteem nor will it diminish love.

Fusion, as I mentioned earlier, is the enemy of intimacy. A relationship which is too close can be destructive. It can wipe out the unusual and unique qualities of both people, or it can allow one partner to take over, manage or manipulate the other.

In becoming intimate with someone, we must realize that not only are none of us perfect, but most of us are terribly flawed. However, those flaws are sometimes the very things that attract us to another. Like a template and a form, the lack in one fits the presence in another. When flawed people become intimate, they can strengthen each other, and the result may be stronger than either.

The Secret of Taking a Chance

In building an intimate relationship, trust is the major structural factor. Once you have trust you can risk emotional honesty. You can open yourself to your partner and reveal the good and the bad within you.

By the same token, your partner can reveal his weaknesses as well as his strengths. Unfortunately if we wait for mutual trust to occur on its own initiative, we may never live to find it!

Instead of waiting, we *have* to take the risk. We *have* to reveal some part of our inner self. When we reveal ourselves, we must be sure we can stand up to that revelation and its consequences. We must be sensitive enough to know whether the risk is worth taking.

A woman involved with a man who is destructive to her must realize that if she trusts him enough to risk telling him her own needs, he may use that knowledge to try to destroy her. Is the risk worth it? Or will the exposure be so damaging that intimacy will become impossible?

Too often people who are searching for intimacy are advised that self-knowledge is the total answer, the panacea for all emotional problems. "If you are secure in yourself," they're told, "no one can hurt you." The truth is that all of us can be hurt and rejected. Someone who cannot be hurt or who fails to suffer from rejection is so rigid that he has blocked off all understanding of himself. He has stopped feeling.

The act of being hurt, the sense of your own vulnerability, must also be recognized as the act of being alive. It is true that many people will hurt you once you begin to take risks, but you can ride out the hurt and overcome it if you keep in mind the fact that your life will improve with the chances you are taking. It is up to you to judge whether any hurt is worth the possible pain.

Once you begin the journey to intimacy, you should be prepared for the pitfalls just as you must be prepared for the feelings of happiness and sorrow, anger and compassion, joy and grief.

The intensity and the variety of the emotions we feel and express are indications of the fullness of our lives. Because we are afraid to risk, we settle for mediocre lives—which are really quiet desperation.

If you cannot hate, you cannot love. If you cannot cry and grieve, you cannot feel joy because all these emotions exist by comparison.

Becoming intimate is not only a way of becoming alive, it is also a life-long process. One solitary risk will not work wonders. To make life work, you have to risk again, and again, and again.

All of this is a difficult, challenging task but you must always keep in mind the fact that if you settle for a life with little or no intimacy, your life will be measurably impoverished as time goes by.